ANY TIME'S A PARTY!

ANY TIME'S A PARTY!

CREATIVE MENUS FOR ENTERTAINING THROUGHOUT THE YEAR

by
Barbara Cook, Grace Toler, and Creath Fowler

QUAIL RIDGE PRESS

To the men who love us, care about us, are interested in what we do, who like for us to entertain, and are definitely the most enthusiastic over "our cooking," we lovingly dedicate this cookbook to Billy, Bill, Jr. and John; to Noel, Noel III and Ward; and to Gibbs, Gibbs, Jr. and Donald.

CONTENTS

PREFACE

The goal of every aspiring host or hostess is the perfect dinner. Often, however, the biggest problem is not the preparation of the meal, but the choosing of the menu. This cookbook is designed to provide creative menu ideas along with superb recipes for having fun parties anytime of the year.

The occasions for entertaining are endless. Some of these events may be a Super Bowl Party, an Election Night Dinner, a Mexican Fiesta, a Basket Barbeque, a Graduation Luncheon or perhaps a Bon Voyage Party for a friend. Included here are 24 party possibilities (two for each month) along with menus, plus decorating suggestions for each party theme.

We arranged the menus in this cookbook to help the host create the complete dinner. Every facet of the meal was taken into consideration. The foods compliment each other on the basis of agreeability, nutrition, texture, color, and of course, taste. The menus are not only pleasing to the palate, but delightful to the eye.

The recipes come from many different sources. Some are family hand-me-downs, some are treasured recipes of friends, many we devised from noted restaurants throughout the country. Most are our own creations from our southern kitchens—the culmination of years of entertaining . . . and loving it!

Whether you serve on paper plates or with ruffles and flourishes, remember that good food and good times go together. So no matter what time of year or what the occasion, serve an exceptional and memorable meal with a little help from The Party Calendar Cookbook.

Barbara Cook, Grace Toler,
and Creath Fowler

JANUARY

NEW YEAR'S PROGRESSIVE SUPPER

This is a fun-time party to welcome in Father Time with your neighbors and friends. Spread the word and spread the work! Have the salad course at one home, main course at another, and end up with dessert at still another. "Should auld acquaintance be forgot?"

Auld Lang Syne Chicken Spaghetti
Fresh Start Salad Bar
Merry Marinated Vegetables
Garlic Bread
Nostalgic Lemon Ice Box Pie

SUPER BOWL PARTY

A real favorite for the men in your life—and the women will love it because it's finally the end of the season! Plan a casual party with good food, good friends, and good entertainment. Serve buffet, providing each person with an individual tray for eating around the television.

Official Brunswick Stew
Super Bowl Spinach Salad
Winning Cornbread
Old Timer's Gingerbread with Lemon Sauce

New Year's Progressive Supper

AULD LANG SYNE CHICKEN SPAGHETTI

2 (3½-lb.) chickens
1¾ cups reserved chicken broth
¾ bell pepper, chopped
1 medium onion, chopped
4 stalks celery, chopped
4 tablespoons chopped parsley
1 small jar pimentos, chopped

2 cans mushroom soup
1 (4 oz.) can mushrooms,
  chopped
3 cups raw spaghetti, broken
½ teaspoon salt
¼ teaspoon pepper
1 lb. Velveeta cheese, grated

Cook and debone chickens, reserving broth. Cut into bite-sized pieces. Cook vegetables in broth until tender. Cook and drain spaghetti. Mix spaghetti and two-thirds of cheese. Add vegetables, pimentos, soup, mushrooms, chicken, broth and seasonings. Put in two medium-sized casseroles. Cover and refrigerate overnight. Sprinkle remaining cheese over top and bake at 350 degrees for 45 minutes or until bubbly. Serves 12. This casserole freezes well.

FRESH START SALAD BAR

Iceberg lettuce
Romaine lettuce
Shredded purple cabbage
Hard-boiled eggs, finely chopped
Bacos
Sliced bell pepper
Toasted croutons

Chopped green onions.
Sliced cucumber
Sliced radishes
Sliced fresh mushrooms
Cherry or quartered tomatoes
Parmesan cheese
Assorted salad dressings

Wash and drain lettuce. Tear into bite-sized pieces. Mix lettuces and cabbage in large salad bowl. Put other ingredients in small bowls so guests can make the salad of their choice.

MERRY MARINATED VEGETABLES

1 can pickled beets
1 can cut green beans
1 can wax beans

MARINADE:
½ cup sugar
5 tablespoons salad oil

DRESSING:
1 cup sour cream
½ cup mayonnaise
¼ cup chives

1 can sliced carrots
1 medium onion, sliced
1 small green pepper, sliced

5 tablespoons vinegar
Salt and pepper to taste

2 tablespoons vinegar
½ teaspoon salt
Dash of pepper

Drain all canned ingredients except beets in a colander. In a bowl, alternate drained vegetables with onions and green pepper. Marinate covered overnight in the refrigerator in marinade mixture. Right before serving, drain marinade and fold in drained beets. Serve with dressing which has been placed in a glass bowl in the center of a platter surrounded by attractively arranged vegetables. Serves 10–12.

GARLIC BREAD

1 loaf French bread
2 cloves garlic, pressed
½ cup butter, melted

1 tablespoon minced parsley
¼ cup grated Parmesan cheese
½ teaspoon paprika

Split loaf in half lengthwise. Place each half, crust down, on baking sheet. Combine garlic and butter and brush over cut surfaces. Mix remaining ingredients and sprinkle over buttered surfaces. Cut in 2" bias slices. Heat on baking sheet at 350 degrees for 12–15 minutes.

NOSTALGIC LEMON ICE BOX PIE

18 Graham cracker squares
½ stick butter, melted
¼ cup sugar
1 can condensed milk

2 egg yolks
Scant ½ cup fresh lemon juice
½ pint whipping cream, whipped
2 tablespoons sugar

A homemade crust makes this pie so delicious! Crush Graham crackers into fine crumbs. Mix with sugar and melted butter. Press in pie plate. Bake 5 mintues in 325-degree oven. Cool. Mix condensed milk, egg yolks and lemon juice until blended. Pour into pie crust and top with whipped cream that has been sweetened with sugar. Regrigerate. For a lighter variation, fold stiffly beaten egg whites into pie mixture.

OFFICIAL BRUNSWICK STEW

1½–2½ chickens
1 lb. beef chuck or stew meat
2 quarts canned tomatoes
3 slices crisp cooked bacon,
  crumbled
½ stick margarine
4 large onions, chopped
5 stalks celery, chopped
Salt and pepper to taste
½ green pepper, chopped

2 slices stale bread, crumbled
2 (10 oz.) pkgs. frozen okra
1–2 cups butter beans
2 medium potatoes, chopped
1 (16-oz.) can creamed corn
1 teaspoon chili powder
Few dashes cinnamon
7 drops Tabasco
¼ teaspoon garlic powder
2 tablespoons Worcestershire

Cover chicken and beef with water in large boiler. Cook until meat comes off bones. Debone and chop chicken and beef into small pieces. Return to broth; add tomatoes and crumbled bacon. Then add margarine, onions, celery, seasonings, green pepper and crumbled bread. Cook for one hour. Add okra and butter beans. Continue cooking 30 minutes, then add potatoes, corn, chili powder, cinnamon, Tabasco, garlic powder and Worcestershire. Stir frequently and simmer another hour. Serve with big chunks of cornbread. Serves 8–10.

SUPER BOWL SPINACH SALAD

2 (10-oz.) pkgs. fresh spinach
6–8 strips crisp cooked bacon,
  crumbled

4 hard-boiled eggs, shredded
Fresh mushrooms, sliced
Croutons

Tear tough stems from fresh spinach leaves. Wash well and return to refrigerator to crisp. When ready to serve, toss gently with remainder of ingredients and the following dressing. This will serve 8–10.

SUPER BOWL SALAD DRESSING

1 cup salad oil
5 tablespoons red wine vinegar
4 tablespoons sour cream
1½ teaspoons salt
½ teaspoon dry mustard

2 tablespoons sugar
Coursely ground pepper
1 tablespoon or more chopped
  fresh parsley
2 cloves garlic, pressed

WINNING CORNBREAD

¾ cup plain cornmeal
¼ cup flour
½ teaspoon baking soda
½ teaspoon baking powder
1 tablespoon sugar

½ teaspoon salt
1 egg
1 cup buttermilk
2–3 tablespoons salad oil
1 tablespoon bacon grease

Mix together all but the last ingredient. Preheat skillet (preferably iron) with bacon grease. Sprinkle small amount of cornmeal in skillet when very hot, then add mixture. Bake in 450-degree oven 10–15 minutes or until top is brown.

OLD TIMER'S GINGERBREAD

½ cup butter
½ cup sugar
2 eggs
½ cup molasses
1½ cups cake flour

1 teaspoon baking soda
1 teaspoon ginger
1 teaspoon allspice
1 teaspoon cinnamon
½ cup buttermilk

Cream butter and sugar. Add eggs, beating well after each egg. Add molasses. Sift flour, soda and spices together. Fold in flour mixture alternately with buttermilk. Bake in square pan 25–30 minutes at 350 degrees. Even more delicious to serve with a dollop of sour cream before topping with Old Timer's Lemon Sauce.

OLD TIMER'S LEMON SAUCE

½ cup sugar
4 teaspoons cornstarch
1 cup hot water
1 egg yolk, beaten

1 teaspoon grated lemon rind
3–4 tablespoons lemon juice
1 tablespoon butter

Mix sugar and cornstarch in saucepan. Gradually add the hot water and blend until smooth. Cook on high heat, stirring until thick. Reduce heat and cook 5–7 minutes until clear. Remove from heat. Add a little of this hot mixture to the beaten egg yolk then stir it in quickly. Cook 2 minutes. Add lemon rind, lemon juice and butter.

FEBRUARY

BON VOYAGE PARTY

Whatever the destination, everyone enjoys having a big send-off. Ask your travel agent for posters and brochures. Attire for the evening—cruise line clothes. Use a plastic boat for your centerpiece surrounded by greenery, and red, white and blue balloons. Stick a small plastic flag (available at party stores) in one of the shrimp on each plate. Inspiration increases if you know your geography.

Caribbean Shrimp A La Grace
Toasted Parmesan Squares
Tomato Soup Salad
Captain's Potatoes
Beans Anchored in Bacon
Royal Copenhagen Orange Slice Cake

SWEETHEART'S SUPPER

Hearts, candles, and flowers in red and white make a striking setting for a very special seated dinner. Use individual Valentines as place cards. Garnish the asparagus with tiny cut-out pimento hearts and pass Valentine candy with after dinner coffee.

Essence of Tomato Soup
Beaux's Beef Stroganoff
Romantic Raspberry Salad
Cupid's Asparagus Spears
Refrigerator Rolls
Sweetheart Strawberry Meringues

Bon Voyage Party

CARIBBEAN SHRIMP A LA GRACE

STUFFING:

4 stalks celery, chopped	1 lb. lump crabmeat, picked
4 green onions, chopped	Salt and pepper to taste
2 small garlic cloves, crushed	1 egg
2 tablespoons cooking oil	2 tablespoons Durkee's sauce
½ loaf whole wheat bread	2 tablespoons Worcestershire

Saute celery, onion and garlic in oil over low heat till slightly browned. Soak bread in small amount of water. Squeeze out most of water and add bread to vegetable mixture. Add crabmeat, stirring well over low heat. Season. Add egg to mixture, stirring till well blended. Add Durkee's and Worcestershire. Stir well and remove from heat. Serves 6.

TO STUFF SHRIMP:

30 large, raw shrimp with tail sections on, if possible	2 tablespoons melted butter
	2 tablespoons water

Slit shrimp down center of back almost through. Put butter and water into large baking pan. Carefully place rounded portions of stuffing into slit. Place shrimp, stuffed side up, close together in pan. Bake in preheated 375-degree oven 15–20 minutes or until shrimp are tender.

SAUCE:

1 stick butter	¼ cup sherry
3 tablespoons Worcestershire	Juice of 1 lemon

Simmer all together in saucepan for about 8 minutes. Pour over baked, stuffed shrimp and serve hot. Serves 6 elegantly.

TOASTED PARMESAN SQUARES

Sliced bread	Parmesan cheese
Butter	

Trim bread and cut into fourths. Dip in melted butter and roll in Parmesan cheese. Toast in 250-degree oven until brown and crisp, about 15–20 minutes.

TOMATO SOUP SALAD

1 (3 oz.) box lemon gelatin
1 cup boiling water
1 can tomato soup, undiluted
3 dashes Tabasco
½ teaspoon Worcestershire
1 (3-oz.) bar cream cheese

½ cup mayonnaise
½ cup chopped bell pepper
½ cup chopped celery
2 teaspoons onion juice
½ cup chopped pecans

Add gelatin to boiling water, stirring until dissolved. Add tomato soup, Tabasco and Worcestershire. Cut cream cheese in pieces and add to gelatin. Stir until mostly dissolved. Add other ingredients and stir in thoroughly. Chill until set. Serves 8.

CAPTAIN'S POTATOES

8 baking potatoes
½ cup milk
½ stick butter

Seasoned salt and pepper
8 tablespoons grated Cheddar
cheese

Bake foil-wrapped potatoes in a 350-degree oven for 1½ hours. Heat milk and butter in small saucepan until butter is melted. Carefully cut a top section off of each potato. Scoop out insides into a mixing bowl. Beat milk, butter and potatoes with a mixer. Season and mix another minute. Stuff potatoes back into shells, place on baking pan and heat at 350 degrees for 15–20 minutes or until heated throughout. Sprinkle each potato with grated Cheddar cheese and heat till cheese melts.

BEANS ANCHORED IN BACON

1 (16-oz.) can whole string beans
3 strips bacon

Salt and pepper to taste
½ bottle Kraft Catalina dressing

Drain beans and divide into 6 equal portions. Cut bacon strips in half. Wrap each portion of beans with ½ strip bacon, secure with toothpick. Sprinkle with salt and pepper to taste. Marinate with dressing overnight. Bake in moderate oven for 30 minutes. Serves 6.

ROYAL COPENHAGEN ORANGE SLICE CAKE

1 cup margarine
2 cups sugar
4 eggs
1 teaspoon baking soda
½ cup buttermilk
3½ cups flour

1 lb. chopped dates
1 lb. orange slices, chopped
2 cups nuts, chopped
1 can coconut
1 cup fresh orange juice
2 cups powdered sugar

Cream margarine and sugar until smooth; add eggs one at a time, beating well after each addition. Dissolve soda in buttermilk and add to creamed mixture. Place flour in large bowl. Add dates, orange slices, nuts and coconut. Stir to coat each piece and add to creamed mixture. This makes a very stiff dough that should be mixed with hands. Put in greased and floured 13 x 8 x 2" pan. Bake 2½–3 hours at 250 degrees. Combine orange juice and powdered sugar and pour over hot cake. Let stand overnight.

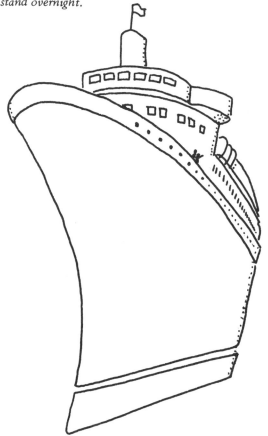

Sweetheart's Supper

ESSENCE OF TOMATO SOUP

1 quart canned tomatoes	1 diced green pepper
¾ cup diced celery	3 whole cloves
½ cup diced carrots	1 teaspoon whole peppercorns
1 small diced onion	1 teaspoon salt
A few twigs of parsley	Dash of cayenne
2 bouillon cubes	Dash of mace

Put tomatoes in saucepan and add vegetables and seasonings. Simmer 45—55 minutes until vegetables are cooked. Strain but do not force vegetables through sieve, as the tomato essence should be clear. Reheat and serve hot in bouillon cups. If you like soup with a little more body, blend, rather than strain, for a few seconds. One of Gibb's favorites!

BEAUX'S BEEF STROGANOFF

2 lbs. round steak	½ teaspoon salt
4 tablespoons butter	¼ teaspoon pepper
2 large onions, chopped	1 (10-oz.) can beef bouillon,
1 clove garlic, minced	undiluted
½ lb. fresh mushrooms or	¼ cup dry white wine
2 (3-oz.) cans sliced mushrooms	2 teaspoons Worcestershire
3 tablespoons flour	Several dashes Tabasco
2 teaspoons meat extract paste	2 (8-oz.) cartons sour cream
½ (6-oz.) can tomato paste	1 (16-oz.) pkg. egg noodles

Trim fat from beef and cut crosswise into ½" slices. Melt butter in a large skillet; add beef and sear quickly on all sides. Turn heat down, cover and simmer 20 minutes. Remove meat from skillet, then saute onions in remaining butter. Add garlic and mushrooms and saute for a few minutes. Add remaining ingredients except sour cream and noodles, and put meat back in pan. Simmer one hour. Add sour cream and heat, but do not boil. Serve over hot cooked noodles. Serves 6—8.

ROMANTIC RASPBERRY SALAD

2¼ cups boiling water
1 large pkg. raspberry gelatin
2 (10 oz.) pkgs. frozen raspberries

1 teaspoon lemon juice
1 cup applesauce

Dissolve gelatin in boiling water. Add the raspberries which have been defrosted. Add lemon juice and applesauce. Congeal.

ROMANTIC TOPPING

½ pint sour cream

22 miniature marshmallows

Mix together 24 hours in advance of using as topping on salad. This salad is a beautiful red-and-white Valentine color and would be even more romantic in a heart-shaped mold.

CUPID'S ASPARAGUS SPEARS

2 cups green asparagus spears
½ cup wine vinegar
6 tablespoons sugar
6 tablespoons water

1 teaspoon salt
6 whole cloves
2 sticks cinnamon
1 teaspoon celery seed

Bring everything to a boil except asparagus. Strain then pour over drained asparagus. Put in refrigerator in tightly closed plastic container and let marinate overnight. Serves 6.

REFRIGERATOR ROLLS

2 cups sweet milk
½ cup shortening
½ cup sugar
1 envelope yeast
2 tablespoons water

4 cups flour (approximately)
1 teaspoon salt
½ teaspoon baking soda
½ teaspoon baking powder

Mix milk, shortening and sugar. Heat to boiling, remove from heat and cool to lukewarm. Dissolve yeast in water and add to mixture. Add 2 cups flour or enough to make a stiff batter. Let stand 1 hour covered in a warm place. Punch dough down and add additional flour, salt, soda and baking powder. Put mixture in a plastic sack and refrigerate overnight. Roll out and shape rolls as needed. Bake at 400 degrees for 12 minutes or until brown. Yields 4 dozen.

SWEETHEART STRAWBERRY MERINGUES

3 egg whites	1 cup sifted granulated sugar
1 teaspoon vanilla	Vanilla ice cream
¼ teaspoon cream of tartar	Fresh strawberries, sliced and
Dash of salt	sweetened

Have egg whites at room temperature. Add vanilla, cream of tartar and salt. Whip to soft peaks. Gradually add sugar, beating till very stiff peaks form and sugar is dissolved. If you want these tinted pink, add a few drops of red food coloring. Cover a baking sheet with plain, ungreased brown paper. Draw 8 circles or heart shapes about 3½ inches in diameter. Spread each with 1/8 of the mixture. Using back of spoon, shape into shells, being sure indentions will hold ice cream. Bake at 275 degrees 1 hour. For crisper meringues, turn off heat and let dry in oven with door closed another hour. Immediately before serving, fill each meringue with ice cream and top with prepared strawberries.

MARCH

SENTIMENTAL JOURNEY ANNIVERSARY DINNER

Since an anniversary is a very special day, mark the milestone by going the extra mile. Make this a formal affair with shiny silver, sparkling crystal, and gleaming china. Ribbon printed with the couple's names and date of their wedding is available rather inexpensively, and makes a nice added touch to your decorations. Have a camera ready for later memories.

French Onion Soup
Beef Bourguignon
Milestone Marinated Tomatoes
Spinach Souffle
Love Knot Rolls
Golden Cup Custard

ST. PATRICK'S DAY SHINDIG

To please any Irishman, the color scheme will naturally be green and white. Fill a green foil paper derby with flowers for your centerpiece. Make shamrock place cards. For an added touch, put sprigs of parsley all around the oyster shells. And the wearin 'o the green keeps Irish eyes smiling!

Creath's Oysters Rockefeller
Shamrock Salad
Green Fettucine
Mr. Jigg's Veal Parmigiana
French Bread
Emerald Pie

19

Sentimental Journey Anniversary Dinner

FRENCH ONION SOUP

3 tablespoons butter	3 tablespoons flour
1 tablespoon cooking oil	2 quarts hot beef bouillon
6 cups thinly sliced yellow onions	1 cup red wine
1 teaspoon salt	1 bay leaf
½ teaspoon sugar	½ teaspoon sage

Melt butter and oil in large heavy saucepan. Add sliced onions and stir. Cover and cook over moderately low heat 15–20 minutes, stirring occasionally until onions are translucent. Raise heat and stir in salt and sugar. Cook, stirring constantly till onions have turned golden brown. Lower heat, stir in flour and add a bit more butter. Cook slowly, stirring, for 2 minutes. When lightly browned, remove from heat and pour in a cup of hot bouillon, stirring with a wire whisk to blend. Add rest of bouillon, wine, bay leaf and sage and simmer 40 minutes. Season to taste with salt and pepper. If not serving immediately, cool uncovered, then cover and refrigerate.

TO SERVE:

1 loaf French bread	Parmesan and Gruyere cheese

Slice French bread in 8 slices about ¾" thick. Toast slowly in 250-degree oven until dry, about 20 minutes. Put in soup bowls and grate cheeses over bread. Ladle hot soup into bowls and serve immediately.

MILESTONE MARINATED TOMATOES

1 teaspoon salt	1 cup salad oil
1 teaspoon paprika	2 garlic buttons, pressed
½ teaspoon sugar	¼–½ cup bleu cheese, crumbled
½ teaspoon dry mustard	4 tomatoes, peeled and sliced
5 tablespoons tarragon vinegar	

Combine all ingredients except bleu cheese and tomatoes in a jar. Cover tightly and shake until thoroughly mixed. Add bleu cheese. Pour over tomatoes. Marinate in refrigerator several hours before serving.

BEEF BOURGUIGNON

4 slices bacon
3 lbs. round steak, cut in
 1-inch cubes
2–3 cups dry, red wine
½ (10½-oz.) can beef bouillon
1 tablespoon tomato paste
½ teaspoon thyme
1 teaspoon salt
Freshly ground pepper

1 bay leaf
2 cloves garlic, minced
½ lb. fresh mushrooms, chopped
 or 1 (4-oz.) can mushrooms,
 drained, reserve liquid
1–2 tablespoons butter
12 small boiling onions
Parsley
Noodles or baked rice

Fry bacon in heavy skillet till crisp. Crumble into large casserole. In fat left in skillet, brown beef on all sides. Pour into casserole. Deglaze skillet with a little of the wine and pour in casserole. Add bouillon, tomato paste, thyme, salt, pepper, bay leaf and garlic. Pour in enough wine to almost cover meat. Cover and bake at 300 degrees for 3–4 hours, till meat is tender. If liquid cooks down, add more wine.

Next saute mushrooms in butter for 3–4 minutes. Peel onions and simmer in a little beef broth until tender, about 20 minutes. Save broth from onions. When meat is done, drain off gravy and add to it the liquid from cooking onions and any leftover mushroom liquid. Thicken with paste made by creaming 1 tablespoon butter with 1 tablespoon flour; gradually blend a little of the hot liquid into flour, then pour into gravy.

Now combine meat with onions and mushrooms and pour gravy over all; heat thoroughly. Sprinkle with minced parsley. Serve over cooked noodles or baked rice with almonds. Serves 6–8.

SPINACH SOUFFLE

¼ cup margarine
¼ cup flour
¾ cup milk
Dash of pepper
½ lb. Velveeta cheese, cubed

1 (10-oz.) pkg. frozen chopped
 spinach, cooked and drained
6 strips fried bacon, crumbled
1 tablespoon chopped onion
4 eggs, separated

Melt margarine over medium heat. Add flour, milk and pepper, stirring till smooth. Add Velveeta cheese; stir until melted. Remove from heat. Stir in well-drained spinach, bacon and finely chopped onion. Gradually add slightly beaten egg yolks; cool. Fold into stiffly beaten egg whites; pour into 1½-quart souffle dish. Bake at 350 degrees for 45 minutes. Serves 8.

LOVE KNOT ROLLS

2 envelopes yeast	6–7 cups flour
2 cups lukewarm water	3 tablespoons cooking oil
¾ cup sugar	2 eggs
1 teaspoon salt	Melted butter as needed

Dissolve yeast in water. Add sugar and salt and stir well. Add 2 cups of the flour and oil and mix. Add 2 more cups of flour and the eggs. Mix well again. Add 2 more cups of flour. You may need to add up to 1 more cup of flour to get dough correct consistency. Cover and let rise in a warm place for 1½ hours. Turn out on floured board and knead for about a minute. Roll out for rolls and cut with a cutter. Fold over in pocketbook fashion, brushing with melted butter, and place in greased pan. Cover with towel and let rise until double in size, about 2 hours. Bake in 400-degree oven for 10 minutes. Makes 4 dozen large rolls. These may be frozen in the pan—allow more time to rise.

GOLDEN CUP CUSTARD

CARMELIZED SUGAR:

1 cup granulated sugar	¼ cup very hot water

Heat sugar in heavy pan over very low heat. Stir constantly for 8–10 minutes until sugar is melted and straw colored. Remove pan from heat and add water very slowly. Return pan to low heat another 8–10 minutes stirring constantly until sugar mixture is color of maple syrup. Remove from heat. Put caramel syrup in bottom of 6 custard cups.

CUSTARD:

2 cups milk	5 egg yolks
½ cup sugar	½ teaspoon vanilla
Few dashes salt	Nutmeg

Preheat oven to 300 degrees. Blend together the milk, sugar and salt. Beat egg yolks well and add to milk mixture. Always add a little of the hot mixture to egg yolks, stirring constantly, before adding eggs to hot milk mixture. Blend well and add vanilla. Pour into custard cups with caramel syrup in them. Dust with nutmeg. Place cups in a pan of hot water. Bake 30 minutes or until knife inserted into edge of cup comes out clean. The hot water will continue to cook the custards, so remove them from pan and cool on rack. Store covered in refrigerator. To unmold, insert knife around edge of cups.

St. Patrick's Day Shindig

CREATH'S OYSTERS ROCKEFELLER

4 (10-oz.) pkgs. chopped frozen
   spinach, cooked and drained
3 cups celery tops
2½ cups green onion tops, chopped
3 pods garlic, mashed
½ cup fresh parsley, chopped
Juice of 2½ lemons
1 stick butter, melted

16 drops Tabasco
2½ tablespoons Worcestershire
Rock salt and oyster shells
5 (12-oz.) jars raw oysters or
   equal amount in shells
Salt and pepper
Lemon juice and butter
½ cup cracker crumbs

Put spinach, celery tops, onion tops, garlic, parsley, lemon juice, butter and sauces in blender or processor a small amount at a time and blend thoroughly. Put rock salt (ice cream salt) in pie pans and place shells around in pans. (The salt keeps oysters hot a long time.) Put raw oysters in shells and sprinkle with salt, pepper and lemon juice. Cover with spinach mixture then with cracker crumbs. Dot with butter and bake in 375–400 degree oven 15 minutes. Serve with French bread. Serves 6.

SHAMROCK SALAD

4 cups torn lettuce
2 medium tomatoes, wedged
1 small cucumber, thinly sliced
¼ cup sliced radishes
2 tablespoons chopped green onions

Croutons
Bacos or diced, cooked bacon
Grated Parmesan cheese
Good Season's Cheese-Garlic
   dressing

Place lettuce in salad bowl. Arrange next 4 ingredients over. Before serving, toss salad with croutons, Bacos and Parmesan cheese. Toss with dressing. Serves 6.

GREEN FETTUCINE

1 (12-oz.) pkg. spinach noodles
½ cup butter or margarine
¾ cup heavy cream
1¼ cups grated Parmesan cheese

¼ teaspoon salt
Dash pepper
2 tablespoons or more chopped
   parsley

Cook and drain noodles. Keep warm. To make Alfredo sauce, heat butter and cream in saucepan till butter is melted. Remove from heat. Add 1 cup Parmesan cheese, salt and pepper. Stir until smooth. Add to warm noodles, tossing until well coated. Sprinkle with remaining cheese and parsley. Serve at once. Serves 6.

MR. JIGG'S VEAL PARMIGIANA

1 lb. thin veal cutlets	*Tomato Sauce*
2 eggs, beaten	1 (8-oz.) pkg. Mozzarella cheese,
1 cup seasoned dry bread crumbs	sliced
½ cup olive or salad oil	¼ cup grated Parmesan cheese

Wipe veal with damp paper towels. Dip cutlets in eggs, then in bread crumbs. In skillet, heat ¼ cup oil. Brown veal slices on both sides a few at a time adding more oil as needed. Remove to a 10 x 6" baking dish. Add half the Tomato Sauce and half the cheese. Repeat layers, ending with Parmesan cheese. Cover with foil. Bake 30 minutes, or until bubbly. Serves 6.

TOMATO SAUCE

2 tablespoons olive or salad oil	¾ teaspoon salt
½ cup chopped onion	½ teaspoon dried oregano
1 clove garlic, crushed	¼ teaspoon dried basil
1 (1-lb.) can Italian tomatoes,	¼ teaspoon pepper
undrained	1 teaspoon Worcestershire
2 teaspoons sugar	

In hot oil in skillet, saute onion and garlic till clear. Add remaining ingredients. Mix well, mashing tomatoes with fork. Bring to boiling, then lower heat. Simmer, covered, 10 minutes.

EMERALD PIE

1 envelope unflavored gelatin	1 teaspoon lime rind, grated
¼ cup cold water	4 egg whites, beaten stiffly with
½ cup sugar	½ cup sugar
½ cup fresh lime juice	20 chocolate wafers, crushed
¼ teaspoon salt	¼ cup butter, melted
4 egg yolks, beaten	½ pint whipping cream, whipped
1 drop green food coloring	1 square semi-sweet chocolate

Soak gelatin in water. In double boiler, cook sugar, lime juice, salt, and beaten egg yolks until consistency of custard. Add coloring and grated lime rind. When custard begins to congeal, whip with wire whisk until fluffy. Fold in egg whites carefully. Make pie shell by combining wafers and melted butter. Press into a 9" pie pan. Pour in filling and chill. Top with thin layer of whipped cream and shave chocolate over. Beautiful!

APRIL

EASTER FAMILY DINNER

Put an Easter bonnet on your dining room table—a large straw hat (or Easter basket) filled with a bouquet of spring flowers. Dyed eggs with names on them serve as attractive place cards. Go all out to make this a family affair.

Easter Sunrise Ham
Temptation Waldorf Salad
Spring Broccoli With Lemon Rain
Cheese Casserole
Orange-Glazed Garden Carrots
In-A-Hurry Rolls
Hummingbird Cake

JUST-BEFORE-TAXES PARTY

A good excuse to get together and have a fun time before Uncle Sam gets his due. A gay and happy spirit should prevail with no melancholy overtones, as we exercise our privilege to pay taxes. Give a prize for the guest who comes looking the most broke. Use oilcloth tablecloths and foil pie pans for plates.

Deadline Chicken Singapore
Extravagant Asparagus Salad
Spinach Stuffed Squash
In-The-Red Tomatoes
Everlasting Whole Wheat Rolls
Bottom Line Chocolate Mousse

Easter Family Dinner

EASTER SUNRISE HAM

1 (14–16 lb.) ham, bone in
1 (6-oz.) can pineapple slices,
  juice reserved

Cherries
Brown sugar and mustard
Cloves

Cut most of fat off ham. Make a coating of equal amounts of fruit juice and brown sugar. Add mustard to taste. Coat ham with mixture. Bake at 250 degrees uncovered about 6 hours, basting frequently. Score ham and place a clove in each cross. Place pineapple slices with cherries inside over ham. Bake another 30–40 minutes.

TEMPTATION WALDORF SALAD

1½ cups diced peeled apples
1 cup diced celery
½ cup chopped pecans

¼ cup raisins
½ cup mayonnaise
Dash salt

Mix all ingredients together and serve on lettuce leaves. Serves 6.

SPRING BROCCOLI WITH LEMON RAIN

2 (10-oz.) boxes frozen broccoli
  spears
½ stick real butter

Salt
Juice of 1 large lemon
Toasted almond slivers

Microwave broccoli in boxes on high for 14 minutes. Let sit in boxes 5 minutes. Or cook conventionally and drain. Melt butter and pour over broccoli which has been put in serving dish. Squeeze juice of lemon over broccoli and salt lightly. Fold gently. Sprinkle with almond slivers.

CHEESE CASSEROLE

10 slices white bread, crust
  removed
3 tablespoons butter, softened
1 lb. sharp cheese, grated
4 eggs, slightly beaten
2 cups milk

1 teaspoon salt
2 teaspoons brown sugar
½ teaspoon dry mustard
1 teaspoon Worcestershire
Dash Tabasco
½ teaspoon minced onion

Cut each slice of bread into 4 pieces. Butter lightly on one side. Layer bread and cheese in buttered casserole dish deep enough to leave 1½ inches from top. Beat eggs and mix with milk and remainder of ingredients. Pour over bread and cheese. Cover and refrigerate overnight. Bring to room temperature before baking at 350 degrees for one hour or until firm and slightly brown. If mixture seems dry when taken out of refrigerator, add a little more milk to make moist. Serves 8.

ORANGE-GLAZED GARDEN CARROTS

1½ lbs. baby carrots, pared   ¼ teaspoon salt
1½ cups water   Few dashes of mace
1 tablespoon butter   Freshly ground pepper
2 tablespoons brown sugar   ¾ cup orange juice
1½ teaspoons cornstarch

Put carrots, sliced diagonally in ½-inch slices, in large saucepan. Add water. Bring to boil, reduce heat and simmer until crisp-tender, about 9 minutes. Drain. Melt butter over low heat; stir in sugar, cornstarch and seasonings. Cook and stir 1 minute; add orange juice slowly. Cook, stirring constantly until thick. Pour over drained carrots.

IN-A-HURRY ROLLS

1¼ cups milk   ¼ cup water
2½ tablespoons sugar   2 envelopes yeast
1½ teaspoons salt   3¼ cups sifted flour
¼ cup shortening

Scald milk. Stir in sugar, salt, and shortening. Cool to lukewarm. Place warm water in large mixing bowl and add yeast. Stir until dissolved. Add lukewarm milk mixture and flour. Stir only to mix flour well. Fill well-greased muffin pans half full. Cover and let rise in warm place until doubled in bulk—about 35—45 minutes. Bake in 425-degree oven till brown—about 15 minutes. Serve immediately. Makes 18.

HUMMINGBIRD CAKE

3 cups flour   1½ cups salad oil
2 cups sugar   1½ teaspoons vanilla
1 teaspoon salt   1 (8-oz.) can crushed pineapple,
1 teaspoon soda   undrained
1 teaspoon cinnamon   2 cups chopped bananas
3 eggs beaten   1 cup chopped pecans

Sift together flour, sugar, salt, soda and cinnamon. Add eggs and oil, stirring until dry ingredients are moistened. Do not beat. Stir in vanilla, pineapple, bananas and pecans. Spoon batter into 3 well-greased and floured 9"-cake pans. Bake in 350-degree oven 25—30 minutes. Cool in pans 10 minutes. Spread with frosting when cool.

HUMMINGBIRD FROSTING

2 (8-oz.) bars cream cheese,   2 (1-lb.) boxes powdered sugar
  softened   2 teaspoons vanilla
1 cup butter, softened   1 cup pecans, chopped

Combine all ingredients and beat until fluffy.

Just-Before-Taxes Party

DEADLINE CHICKEN SINGAPORE

1 (4-lb.) chicken, or 3 whole
   chicken breasts, split
Few dashes salt
¼ teaspoon pepper
½ teaspoon paprika
6 tablespoons butter
1 (4-oz.) can sliced mushrooms

1 (No. 303) can artichoke hearts
1 can water chestnuts
3 tablespoons flour
¾ cup chicken broth
1 tablespoon soy sauce
3 tablespoons sherry
¼ teaspoon rosemary

Cut chicken into pieces and season. Place 4 tablespoons butter in skillet and saute mushrooms. Arrange artichoke hearts and water chestnuts around chicken. Sprinkle flour over mushrooms; stir in broth, soy sauce, sherry and rosemary. Cook 8–10 minutes. Pour over chicken, cover and bake 1½ hours at 350 degrees. Delicious over rice. Serves 8.

EXTRAVAGANT ASPARAGUS SALAD

1 lb. fresh asparagus spears or
   1 (16-oz.) can asparagus
6 slices bacon
¼ cup wine vinegar
2 teaspoons sugar

Dash of salt
Dash of pepper
2 green onions, chopped
Shredded lettuce
2 hard-cooked eggs, sliced

Cook asparagus in boiling salted water 8–10 minutes, or drain canned asparagus. Cook bacon until crisp. Remove bacon, drain and crumble; set aside. Add vinegar, sugar, salt, pepper and onions to skillet drippings. Add asparagus; heat through. Arrange asparagus on bed of lettuce in 6 salad bowls; top with egg slices. Pour hot bacon dressing over each salad. Sprinkle with bacon. Makes 6 servings.

EVERLASTING WHOLE WHEAT ROLLS

1 quart sweet milk
1 cup lard or shortening
1 cup sugar
2 envelopes dry yeast

7–7½ cups whole wheat flour
1 tablespoon salt
1 teaspoon baking soda
1¼ teaspoons baking powder

Let milk, lard and sugar come to a boil; set aside. When just warm, dissolve the yeast in the mixture and sift in enough flour to get to the consistency of cake batter (about 1 heaping quart). Let set 2 hours in warm place. Sift in salt, soda, and baking powder. Add flour enough to make a dough. Roll out a portion and make into rolls. Store remainder, well-greased, covered, in refrigerator. Let dough rise (about 40 minutes) and bake in 350-degree oven. Total recipe makes 80–100 rolls.

SPINACH STUFFED SQUASH

6 nice-sized crookneck yellow
   summer squash
1 teaspoon sugar
2 boxes frozen chopped spinach

1 (8-oz.) bar cream cheese
1 stick margarine
Pepperidge Farm bread crumbs
Seasoned salt

Parboil whole squash in water with sugar until fork tender (about 25 minutes). Drain well. Cook spinach according to package directions. Drain thoroughly. Or microwave in boxes 14 minutes. Melt margarine and cream cheese in hot spinach. Add seasoned salt and bread crumbs. Cut squash in half lengthwise and scrape out insides, leaving shell. You may add scrappings to spinach mixture if desired. Spoon into squash halves. Make early in day and heat in 325-degree oven when ready to serve—about 15 minutes. Makes 12 halves.

IN-THE-RED TOMATOES

3 large tomatoes, halved
1 teaspoon salt
Dash of pepper

½ cup finely chopped onion
½ teaspoon basil
1 tablespoon butter or margarine

Sprinkle tomatoes with salt and pepper. Combine onion and basil and sprinkle on tomatoes. Top with butter and broil 10 minutes. Serves 6.

BOTTOM LINE CHOCOLATE MOUSSE

1 (12-oz.) pkg. chocolate morsels
4 eggs
4 tablespoons strong hot coffee

6 tablespoons rum or orange
   liquour
1½ cups boiling milk

Put everything in blender or processor and blend for a couple of minutes. Place in individual dishes. Chill for 8 hours or overnight. Even more delectable to top with whipped cream. Serves 8.

MAY

GRADUATION LUNCHEON

An accomplishment worth celebrating! Use a mock diploma for your invitations to the graduates. Decorate with crepe paper and tassles of school colors. As a memento of the occasion, give each guest an address book to keep in touch.

Elegant Chicken Broccoli Crepes
Circumstance Salad with "Pompy" Seed Dressing
Broiled Tomato Parmesan
Cum Laude Pie

MOTHER'S DAY TRIBUTE

Mom's deserve special recognition. A luncheon lovingly prepared and graciously served befits her royal station in life—make her a Queen-For-A-Day! Have the children make a crown for her to wear during lunch. And give her a personal gift she doesn't need.

Gazpacho
Queen-For-A-Day Crabmeat
Mandarin Memory Salad
Terrific Tomatoes
No-Trouble Rolls
Lemon Angel Pie

Graduation Luncheon

ELEGANT CHICKEN BROCCOLI CREPES

2 eggs
Few dashes salt
1 cup flour

1¼ cups milk, plus more
2 tablespoons melted butter

Combine eggs and salt in mixing bowl. Gradually add flour and milk alternately, beating with mixer till smooth. Beat in melted butter. Refrigerate batter at least an hour. If batter seems too stiff to spread over crepe pan, add more milk. Makes about 16–18 crepes.

CHICKEN BROCCOLI FILLING

6 chicken breasts
2 tablespoons butter
2 boxes frozen chopped broccoli
1 cup grated sharp cheese
1 can cream of chicken soup

3 tablespoons milk
½ pint sour cream
3 tablespoons sherry
Garlic salt
Paprika

Cook chicken breasts in salted water with chunks of butter. Cool and cut into bite-sized pieces. Cook broccoli and drain well. Combine cheese, soup, milk, sour cream and sherry in double boiler and stir till cheese melts. To assemble crepes, mix chicken, broccoli, and enough cheese sauce together to make a little soupy, as it will dry some in cooking. Fill nicely and sprinkle with garlic salt. Roll each crepe and put tuck side down in baking dish. Pour remaining sauce on top and sprinkle with paprika. Bake in 350-degree oven until warm through and sauce is bubbly, about 15 minutes. Serve each guest at least 2 crepes.

BROILED TOMATO PARMESAN

2 tablespoons melted butter
2 cloves garlic, crushed
¼ cup chopped parsley
½ teaspoon salt

Few dashes pepper
1 cup fresh bread cubes ¼"-square
Parmesan cheese
4 fresh tomatoes, sliced ¾"-thick

Melt butter and add everything to it except cheese and tomatoes. The bread cubes will absorb the butter. Put a dab of mixture on each tomato slice. Sprinkle with Parmesan cheese. Broil 5–6 inches from heat until brown. May fix these day before; cook just before serving.

CIRCUMSTANCE SALAD

Watermelon balls
Cantaloupe balls
Honeydew melon chunks

Sliced bananas
Blueberries, washed and drained
Strawberries, sliced, if large

Fruit may be prepared 24 hours ahead of time with the exception of bananas. This salad may be served either lightly tossed and placed on lettuce leaves on individual plates with dressing poured over; or buffet style by tearing lettuce into bite-sized pieces and mixing with the fruit and tossing with the dressing. This looks lovely served in a glass bowl.

"POMPY" SEED DRESSING

½ cup sugar
3½ tablespoons vinegar
Scant teaspoon salt
Scant teaspoon dry mustard

½ teaspoon prepared onion juice
¾ cup salad oil
1 tablespoon poppy seeds

Mix sugar, salt, vinegar and mustard. Add onion juice. Add oil slowly, beating constantly until thick. Add poppy seeds and mix well. Store covered in refrigerator. This will keep for several days.

CUM LAUDE PIE
(DIVINITY CHOCOLATE NUT PIE)

23 Ritz crackers
3 egg whites
1 cup sugar
1 cup chopped pecans
1 teaspoon vanilla

½ pint whipping cream
2 teaspoons powdered sugar
3 teaspoons instant Bakers
    chocolate
1 square semi-sweet chocolate

Crush or process crackers finely. Beat egg whites until stiff; add sugar and nuts. Add crushed crackers and vanilla. Pour into lightly buttered pie plate. Bake in 325-degree oven 25–30 minutes. Cool. Whip cream, adding powdered sugar and instant chocolate. Cover top of pie with cream. Grate slivers of chocolate on top.

GAZPACHO

2 cans tomato soup
1 soup can water
1½ cups bouillon
1 (46-oz.) can V-8 juice
2 cups finely chopped cucumber
1 cup finely chopped green pepper
½ cup minced onion
½ cup salad or olive oil
4 tablespoons wine vinegar

2 small cloves garlic, minced
1 cup finely chopped celery
4 dashes Tabasco
2 tablespoons lemon juice
½ teaspoon dried basil
1 tablespoon chopped parsley
Salt and pepper
¾ cup croutons

Mix all together and chill the soup 24 hours. Serves 10–12.

QUEEN-FOR-A-DAY CRABMEAT

1 lb. lump crabmeat, picked
Juice of ½ lemon
2 tablespoons butter
1 tablespoon cornstarch
½ pint whipping cream
1 egg yolk

Salt
Sherry to taste
Parmesan cheese
Sharp American cheese, grated
Paprika

Sprinkle crabmeat with lemon juice. Melt butter in saucepan and add crabmeat. Saute 2 minutes. Mix cornstarch with whipping cream and egg yolk and add to crabmeat mixture, stirring until thick. Season with salt. Add sherry to taste (about 3 tablespoons). Pour into buttered casserole or individual remekins. Sprinkle with Parmesan and grated American cheese. Top with sprinkle of paprika. Bake at 350 degrees until heated through and cheese is melted. Serves 4–6.

MANDARIN MEMORY SALAD

1 (10-oz.) pkg. fresh spinach
Toasted almond slivers

2 cans mandarin oranges,
drained

Wash and pick spinach for salad. When ready to serve, toss torn spinach with almond slivers and oranges. Toss with dressing. Serves 6.

MEMORY DRESSING

5 tablespoons sugar
½ teaspoon dry mustard
½ teaspoon salt

3 tablespoons vinegar
¼ teaspoon prepared onion juice
½ cup salad oil

Mix sugar, mustard, salt, and vinegar together. Add onion juice and stir thoroughly. Add oil slowly, beating constantly until thick.

TERRIFIC TOMATOES

Fresh tomatoes
Salt

Parmesan cheese
Italian bread crumbs

Slice tomatoes ¾"-thick. Sprinkle with a little salt, Parmesan cheese and Italian bread crumbs. Broil until cheese melts and bread crumbs slightly brown. Easy and good!

NO-TROUBLE ROLLS

2 cups warm water
1 envelope yeast
½ cup sugar
½ cup powdered milk

¾ cup vegetable oil
1 egg
4 cups self-rising flour

Dissolve yeast in warm water. Add other ingredients and mix well. Grease muffin tins and fill two-thirds full. Let them rise 30 minutes and bake in pre-heated 400-degree oven 15 minutes or until brown. This dough will keep in refrigerator several days. Makes 24.

LEMON ANGEL PIE

½ cup egg whites (4 large)
¼ teaspoon salt
1 teaspoon vinegar

1¼ cups sugar
1 cup whipping cream
2 tablespoons sugar

Beat egg whites until frothy. Add salt and vinegar and beat until stiff. Gradually add sugar, about 2 tablespoons at a time, beating thoroughly after each addition. This takes quite some time—it will be very stiff and glossy. Spread in well-greased and floured 9"-round cake pan, making edges slightly higher than center. Bake in 275-degree oven 1 hour. Remove immediately from pan to prevent sticking. Cool. Whip cream with 2 tablespoons sugar till stiff. Spread half of whipped cream on cool meringue. Then cover with Tart Lemon Filling. Spread over remaining whipped cream. Serve at once or chilled. Guests will ask for this recipe!

TART LEMON FILLING

4 egg yolks, beaten till thick
6 tablespoons sugar

2 teaspoons grated lemon peel
3 tablespoons lemon juice

Gradually add sugar to egg yolks and add lemon peel and juice. Cook over hot water until thick, 5—7 minutes, stirring constantly. Cool.

JUNE

FATHER'S DAY MEN-U

Here's your opportunity to make a big fuss over Dad. On this day his likes and dislikes should be considered. If he likes to eat out-of-doors, by all means do so. Have the dessert ready when he wakes up from his nap!

Papa's Shish-Ka-Bob
Yellow Saffron Rice
Emperor Salad
Monkey Bread
He's No. 1 Bread Pudding with Whiskey Sauce

BRIDESMAID'S LUNCHEON

Usually held the day of the wedding, the bridesmaid's luncheon is a time for reminiscing with members of the wedding party. Use the shade of the bridesmaid's dresses as a color scheme for the luncheon. The bride-to-be takes this opportunity to thank her friends for sharing in this occasion with a remembrance.

Bride's Consomme
Delectable Crabmeat Quiche
Heart-Of-My-Heart Tomato Salad
TLC Asparagus With Lemon Butter Sauce
Bridegroom's Bran Muffins
Blueberry Bouquet Pie

PAPA'S SHISH-KA-BOB

6 ounces beefsteak per person
Bell pepper
Small onions

Mushroom caps
Cherry tomatoes

MARINADE:
½ cup olive oil
1 teaspoon thyme
2 large onions, chopped
2 cloves garlic, minced
2 bay leaves

¼ cup fresh lemon juice
1 cup red wine
Pinch of red pepper
Salt and pepper to taste

Marinate cubed meat in marinade mixture for at least 6 hours. When ready to cook, skewer a piece of meat, bell pepper, onion, and mushroom cap. Repeat for each skewer. You might want to skewer tomatoes separately and cook separately, as they cook faster. When cooking on grill, add hickory chips the last few minutes of cooking. A fun party would be to let everyone make their own shish-ka-bob and cook it to their own taste!

EMPEROR SALAD

1 head iceberg lettuce
1 head Romaine lettuce
1 clove garlic, cut in half
½ cup French dressing
1 raw egg

¼ cup fresh lemon juice
Salt and pepper to taste
½ cup grated Parmesan cheese
1 cup homemade croutons

Rub salad bowl with garlic. Wash, drain, dry and tear lettuces into bite-sized pieces and put in bowl. Add French Dressing. Toss lightly. Break egg onto salad, add lemon juice and toss till no trace of egg can be seen. Add salt, pepper, Parmesan. Add croutons just before serving. If desired add capers, anchovies and/or crisp, crumbled bacon. Serves 8–10.

FRENCH DRESSING

2 teaspoons salt
1 teaspoon sugar
½ teaspoon pepper

1 teaspoon paprika
½ cup apple cider vinegar
1½ cups salad oil

Combine all and shake well in covered jar, or make in blender. Shake again before using. Lemon juice may be used in place of vinegar, especially for fruit salads. Makes 2 cups.

MONKEY BREAD

1 envelope yeast
¾ cup warm water
2½ cups biscuit mix

Dash of salt
5 tablespoons sugar
Melted margarine

Dissolve yeast in water. Combine other ingredients except margarine; mix with yeast. Knead 1 minute on surface sprinkled with extra biscuit mix. Roll out dough. Grease bundt pan with melted margarine. Cut dough into irregular pieces, dipping each piece into margarine, and lay in pan—about 3 layers. Let rise in warm place 1 hour. Bake in preheated 400-degree oven for about 25 minutes.

HE'S NO. 1 BREAD PUDDING

3 eggs, beaten lightly
½ cup sugar
¼ teaspoon salt
¼ teaspoon nutmeg

2 tablespoons melted butter
4 cups scalded milk
1 teaspoon vanilla
5 slices raisin bread

Combine eggs, sugar, salt, nutmeg and butter. Slowly add milk and vanilla. Add raisin bread which has been torn into small pieces and mix well. Pour into greased 2-quart baking dish. Place dish in pan with 1 inch hot water surrounding. Bake at 350 degrees about 1 hour. Serve warm or chilled. Serves 8. This is a "New Orleansy" recipe.

WHISKEY SAUCE

1 stick butter
1 cup sugar

2 egg yolks, beaten
¼ cup whiskey, or to taste

Melt butter with sugar and add egg yolks. Remove from heat and add whiskey. Serve over bread pudding.

Bridesmaids' Luncheon

BRIDE'S CONSOMME

2 (13-oz.) cans consomme
2 tablespoons lemon juice

Sour cream
Chopped chives

Pour the consomme in a 9"-square pan or 2 ice cube trays and add the lemon juice. Place in freezer to chill 15 minutes or until consistency of unbeaten egg whites. Serve in consomme cups or small bowls topped with chives and a dollop of sour cream. Serves 6.

DELECTABLE CRABMEAT QUICHE

1 lb. white crabmeat
12–16 oz. Swiss cheese
1 cup mayonnaise
1 cup milk
2 beaten eggs
Dash of cayenne pepper

1 bunch green onions with tops,
  finely chopped
1 cup chopped parsley
4 teaspoons flour
¼ teaspoon dry mustard
2 unbaked pie shells

Go over crabmeat finely to check for shells. Grate cheese, mix all ingredients together and pour into pie shells. Bake for 45 minutes at 350 degrees. Serves 12 if both pies are used.

HEART-OF-MY-HEART TOMATO SALAD

1 (8-oz.) bar cream cheese, softened
1 cup homemade mayonnaise
3 (8-oz.) cans tomato sauce
1 small onion, grated

1½ teaspoons lemon juice
Salt to taste
1 teaspoon Worcestershire
3 drops Tabasco

Mash cream cheese and mix with mayonnaise until smooth. Combine tomato sauce with rest of ingredients and add to cream cheese mixture. Freeze in 9"-square pan. Cut into 12 squares when ready to serve.

TLC ASPARAGUS WITH LEMON BUTTER SAUCE

Fresh asparagus (about the size
  of your little finger)
Salt

Real butter
Fresh lemon juice

Handle asparagus carefully, breaking off bottom where it naturally breaks. Discard bottoms. Put freshly washed asparagus in a skillet with salted water to barely cover. Put lid on and steam slowly until tender. Drain and pour freshly squeezed lemon juice and melted butter over attractively arranged spears. Serve immediately.

BRIDEGROOM'S BRAN MUFFINS

6 cups All-Bran cereal
2 cups boiling water
1 cup salad oil
5 cups all-purpose flour
2 teaspoons salt

3 cups sugar
5 teaspoons baking soda
4 eggs, beaten
1 quart buttermilk
2 cups raisins

Combine 2 cups cereal, boiling water and salad oil, mixing well. Set aside. Combine flour, salt, sugar, flour, soda and remaining cereal. Mix together eggs and buttermilk and add to flour mixture. Stir in cereal-oil mixture. Add raisins, if desired. Bake desired number in greased muffin pans at 400 degrees for 15 minutes. Remainder will keep well in covered container in refrigerator up to 6 weeks.

BLUEBERRY BOUQUET PIE

8 oz. cream cheese, softened
¼ cup sugar
Graham cracker crust

1 cup chopped pecans, divided
1 (12-oz.) carton Kool Whip
1 can blueberry pie filling

Blend cream cheese and sugar till creamy. Spread on crust and sprinkle with ½ cup pecans. Spread on a layer of Kool Whip, then the remainder of the pecans. Spread pie filling over this and top with Kool Whip. Refrigerate at least an hour before serving. Makes one large 10" pie or two 7" pies. Serves 8–10.

JULY

JULY 4TH REUNION

A time for patriotism to blaze anew! Many families use this holiday as a time for reunions. Go all out with red, white and blue decorations. Have each family bring a different dish and put it all together for a delicious meal. A clever and pretty way to serve the coleslaw is in a scooped out large head of cabbage.

Firecracker Chicken	Crowder Peas With Okra
Firecracker Barbeque Sauce	Watermelon Rind Pickles
Old Glory Potato Salad	Red, White and Blue Dessert
Anne's Coleslaw	Watermelon

Mama's Commemorative Mayonnaise

NIGHTTIME IN NEW ORLEANS

Set the mood for this party by serving dinner on the patio. Beg, borrow, or rent hurricane lamps and place all around to give a New Orleans atmosphere. Use taped Dixieland music in the background. While preparing for this party, keep in mind that it's cheaper than going to New Orleans!

Crescent City Shrimp Creole
Vieux Carre Salad
French Quarter Garlic Bread
Frozen Creole Dessert Cups or
Royal Street Bananas Foster
Cafe Au Lait

July 4th Reunion

FIRECRACKER CHICKEN

This is a very old recipe from the Mississippi Delta. It is always served on the 4th of July and at dove hunts.

Cut 6 whole chickens into halves. Rub each with salad oil, salt and pepper. Place on a covered charcoal grill skin side down. Brown chickens well to seal juices before adding Firecracker Barbeque Sauce.

FIRECRACKER BARBEQUE SAUCE

1 stick margarine	¼ cup Worcestershire
1 cup salad oil	¼ teaspoon each salt and pepper
1 cup cider vinegar	¼ teaspoon garlic salt
Juice of 6 lemons and peelings	Dash of Tabasco

Mix ingredients together in small saucepan until margarine has melted. Simmer at least 15 minutes. Brush chicken halves with sauce every 15 minutes while cooking slowly on covered grill about 3 hours. The chickens can be cooked ahead of time and put in foil in a 200-degree oven until ready to serve.

OLD GLORY POTATO SALAD

Barbara's husband's secretary, Lillie, is quite renowned for her potato salad. It is a favorite with everyone in his office.

8–9 medium white potatoes	6 hardboiled eggs, chopped
Salt and pepper	¾ cup Rainbow dill pickles,
1½ cups Hellman's mayonnaise	chopped
1 teaspoon mustard	¾ cup Rainbow sweet pickles,
¼ cup Spanish olives	chopped
3 stalks celery, chopped	

Cook potatoes until just tender. Cool, peel and cut into ½-inch cubes. Season and set aside. Mix mayonnaise and mustard together in large bowl. Add chopped olives, celery, eggs and pickles. Add this to potatoes, folding gently, adding more mayonnaise till desired consistency. Store covered in refrigerator. Pretty to decorate with sliced olives and sliced hardboiled eggs. This serves 20.

ANNE'S COLESLAW

Creath's mother-in-law made the best coleslaw anywhere. This was her simple and delicious recipe.

SLAW:

1 small to medium head cabbage, shredded

2 small carrots, shredded

1 small onion cut in thin rings and separated

½ bell pepper, chopped

DRESSING:

¾ cup mayonnaise

1 level teaspoon mustard

1 heaping tablespoon chopped sweet pickle

2 teaspoons salad oil

2 teaspoons white vinegar

½ teaspoon salt

½ teaspoon sugar

Mix all slaw vegetables together, cover and refrigerate. Pour well-mixed dressing over slaw an hour or so before serving. Serves 8.

CROWDER PEAS WITH OKRA

¼ lb. salt meat

2 lbs. shelled crowder peas

2 tablespoons bacon grease

1 clove of garlic

Seasoned salt

15–20 small, tender okra pods

Put salt meat in about 3 cups water and parboil about 15 minutes. Add rinsed and drained crowder peas and season with bacon grease, salt, pepper and garlic. Add seasoned salt to taste. (This is the secret of good crowder peas—keep adding seasoned salt until they have a good flavor.) Cook for 1 hour, boiling gently. Remove garlic clove and place rinsed okra on top of peas. Cook another 30 minutes.

MAMA'S COMMEMORATIVE MAYONNAISE

1 egg

1 tablespoon vinegar

Salt and cayenne pepper to taste

1½ cups salad oil

Mix egg, vinegar, salt and pepper. Beat with electric mixer for about 1 minute. While beating slowly, add oil in a very thin stream until an emulsion is formed and all oil has been used. Serve with a platter of homegrown, sliced tomatoes.

WATERMELON RIND PICKLES

This is my husband's very favorite pickle. In fact, he has several pieces with his lunch every day. I have to make several batches every summer to keep him and friends supplied. It is an old "handed down" (Creath's) recipe from Georgia.

8 lbs. watermelon rind (2 melons)
1 bottle Lilly's Lime (calcium
  hydroxide), get at drug store
¼ box whole ginger
3 pts. cider vinegar

3 pts. water
7½ lbs. sugar
¼ box cinnamon sticks
½ box pickling spices

Cut outer green rind from white part of melon. (The white part is what you pickle, so the thicker, the better.) Trim all red meat from white rind and cut into strips 1" x 2". In a granite or crokery container, place rind, add Lilly's Lime, cover with water and let stand overnight. Next morning rinse, then cover with water. Cook 1 hour in any large container. Rinse again. Cover with water; add ¼ box of whole ginger. Soak another hour. Rinse once more. Mix cider vinegar, water, sugar, cinnamon sticks and pickling spices. Pour mixture over the prepared rind. Cook until clear. It will be quite some time—about 2½ hours. Can and seal—no processing necessary. Makes about 12 delicious pints.

RED, WHITE AND BLUE DESSERT

1 (3-oz.) pkg. strawberry gelatin
1 pint fresh strawberries, sliced
½ cup water
2 envelopes unflavored gelatin
4 tablespoons sugar

1 (16-oz.) container sour cream
1 (3-oz.) pkg. lemon gelatin
1 (9-oz.) pkg. frozen blueberries,
  thawed

Prepare strawberry gelatin as package directs; refrigerate until mixture mounds when dropped from spoon. Fold in sliced strawberries. Pour into 8-cup mold or 9" x 13" Pyrex casserole. Refrigerate "red."

To make "white," put ½ cup water in small saucepan and sprinkle in 2 envelopes unflavored gelatin. Stir over low heat until dissolved. Then stir 2 tablespoons sugar and 2 tablespoons dissolved gelatin into the 16-oz. container of sour cream. Pour "white" into mold over "red." Chill until almost set.

Meanwhile make "blue" by preparing lemon gelatin as package directs. Place ½ cup lemon gelatin and thawed blueberries into blender and blend at low speed. Pour this into remaining lemon gelatin. Stir in remaining unflavored gelatin and 2 remaining tablespoons sugar. Refrigerate separately until mixture mounds when dropped from spoon; pour over "red and white." Refrigerate until firm. Makes 12 beautiful, patriotic and delicious servings!

Nighttime in New Orleans

CRESCENT CITY SHRIMP CREOLE

4 tablespoons flour	1½ cups water
1 cup butter	2 bay leaves
1 large onion, chopped	5 drops Tabasco
3 cloves garlic, minced	Salt and pepper to taste
¾–1 cup chopped celery	1 tablespoon Worcestershire
¾ cup chopped green pepper	½ teaspoon sugar
1 (8-oz.) can tomato sauce	½ teaspoon thyme
1 (8-oz.) can tomato paste	4 cups cooked rice
1 (16-oz.) can tomatoes, mashed	3–4 lbs. raw, peeled shrimp

Saute flour in butter in large skillet very slowly until deep brown but not burned. Add onion, garlic, celery, pepper and green onion and cook until soft. Add tomato sauce, paste, and tomatoes with water and stir thoroughly. Bring to a boil and turn down heat immediately to simmer. Add remainder of ingredients except rice and shrimp. Simmer for 1 hour. Add shrimp and cook 20–25 minutes longer. Serve over rice. Serves 6–8.

VIEUX CARRE SALAD

1 head iceberg lettuce	Cauliflower flowerettes
1 head Romaine lettuce	Fresh yellow squash, sliced
Radishes, sliced	Cucumbers, sliced
Tomatoes, skinned, chopped	1 garlic clove, split
Carrots, sliced	Parmesan cheese
Shallots, sliced	Bacos, salt and pepper
Fresh mushrooms, sliced	Salad dressing
Purple onion, thinly sliced	Croutons

Wash and prepare lettuces and all vegetables except purple onion. Rub wooden salad bowl with cut garlic clove. Put prepared vegetables in bowl and shake Parmesan cheese on generously along with Bacos, salt and pepper. Toss gently with any good oil-based salad dressing. Sprinkle on croutons. Arrange thinly sliced, separated purple onion rings atop salad. Beautiful! Serves 12–15, depending on size of lettuces.

FRENCH QUARTER GARLIC BREAD

1 loaf French bread	2 garlic pods, pressed
1 stick butter	

Soften butter. Mix pressed garlic pods with butter. Slice bread and spread with garlic-butter mixture. Cook French bread uncovered in 400-degree oven until brown, about 10 minutes.

FROZEN CREOLE DESSERT CUPS

2 egg whites, room temperature
½ cup sugar
1 cup whipping cream
2 cups buttermilk
1 teaspoon vanilla

¼ teaspoon baking soda
2 (10-oz.) pkgs. frozen strawberries
3 medium bananas, sliced

Beat egg whites in small bowl at high speed until foamy. Gradually sprinkle in sugar, beating till dissolved and egg whites stand in stiff, glossy peaks. In a large bowl, beat cream till soft peaks form. Reduce mixer speed to low; slowly beat in buttermilk, vanilla, soda and egg whites till well mixed. Spoon mixture into 16 paper or foil-lined 2½" muffin cups. Freeze until firm. Before serving, partially thaw strawberries and toss with sliced bananas. To serve, remove cream from muffin cups and place on serving plate. Top with the fruit.

ROYAL STREET BANANAS FOSTER

5 tablespoons real butter
10 teaspoons brown sugar
4 bananas, halved lengthwise and
crosswise

Ground cinnamon
5 oz. rum
5 teaspoons banana liqueur
Vanilla ice cream

In a flat-bottomed skillet (preferably electric), melt butter; add sugar. Cook bananas in this mixture over medium heat till lightly browned. Turn bananas once. Sprinkle well with cinnamon. Warm the rum and banana liqueur in a small saucepan. Tilt to the side and ignite the liquid. Spoon a little at a time over bananas and let flame die. Serve over ice cream at once.

CAFE AU LAIT

The thick, rich coffee New Orleanians traditionally drink every day is made by mixing 2 parts strong coffee (coffee with chicory preferred) to 1 part scalded milk. Guaranteed to keep your guests awake!

AUGUST

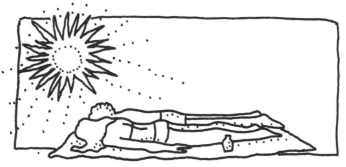

TOO HOT TO COOK

Have this party only if you're desperate to see how your friends vacationed during the summer! This could be your time to do something a little startling or different. Go to little trouble and make it easy on yourself.

Jug Chicken-In-The-Oven
Frosty Pear Salad
Quick 'N Easy Stuffed Potatoes
Lazy Daze Green Beans
Cheese Cubes
Sauced Pound Cake
Summer Mint Tea

BASKET BARBEQUE

Wicker baskets and checkered tablecloths create the desired decor for your informal barbeque. Prepare individual baskets for each couple. Line baskets with napkins and put hamburger dress-ups in individual paper baking cups tied with Saran Wrap and ribbon. At the last minute, add the hot food. Spread blankets on the ground for guests to enjoy a picnic atmosphere.

Barbequed Hamburgers
Basket Barbeque Sauce
Hamburger Dress-ups
Moist Hamburger Buns

Saturday Night Special Beans or
Best Canned Baked Beans
Peach Ice Cream
Buttermilk Pound Cake

Too Hot To Cook

JUG CHICKEN-IN-THE-OVEN

1 stick butter	¼ teaspoon garlic salt
Juice of 1 lemon	1 (2½-lb.) fryer, cut up
¼ cup Worcestershire	Salt and pepper to taste

Mix together butter, lemon juice, Worcestershire and garlic salt. Place over low heat until just melted. Season chicken pieces and place in a shallow baking dish, boney side up. Pour melted mixture over chicken and bake, covered, at 300 degrees 1½ hours, or until tender. Do not turn chicken until ready to put on a serving platter. Serves 4.

FROSTY PEAR SALAD

1 large can pear halves	Bought or homemade Roquefort
Lettuce leaves	dressing

Arrange drained pear halves on lettuce leaves. Top with Roquefort.

QUICK 'N EASY STUFFED POTATOES

1 (8-oz.) pkg. instant mashed	1 carton Lipton onion dip
potato flakes	Grated Cheddar cheese
Water, milk, butter (for mix)	Seasoned salt and pepper

Prepare potatoes according to package directions, except omit 1 cup water and add carton of onion dip. Season with seasoned salt and pepper. Put into 8 foil potato shells. Sprinkle with cheese and bake 15 minutes at 350 degrees.

LAZY DAZE GREEN BEANS

1 (1 lb.) can green beans	1 beef bouillon cube
1 tablespoon dried onion flakes	1½ cups water

Put rinsed and drained beans, onion flakes and bouillon cube in saucepan. Add water and simmer about an hour.

CHEESE CUBES

1 large loaf white bread, unsliced
1 lb. Old English cheese, room temperature

2 sticks butter, room temperature
1 teaspoon Worcestershire

Trim off crust and cut bread into 1" cubes. Combine remaining ingredients thoroughly in mixer. Ice each cube on 5 sides. Place on baking sheet, plain side down. Freeze 15 minutes, transfer to airtight container and return to freezer. When ready to serve, remove desired number and bake on baking sheet at 350 degrees 10 minutes. Do not brown.

SAUCED POUND CAKE

6 (½-inch) slices pound cake
½ cup sugar
4 large egg yolks
1 large whole egg

1 teaspoon vanilla
1 cup milk
¼ cup heavy cream
3 tablespoons brandy

Crumble cake into 6 dessert dishes. Prepare sauce by lightly beating sugar and egg yolks in medium saucepan. Beat the whole egg lightly, then add to sauce with vanilla, milk, cream and mix thoroughly. Set pan over very low heat and cook till mixture thickens, stirring constantly to keep smooth. When custard coats spoon, remove from heat. Add brandy, stir lightly and allow to cool for about 10 minutes. The custard should be warm, not hot, when poured over cake. Serves 6.

SUMMER MINT TEA

To 7 cups boiling water, add 6 teabags, juice of 6 lemons and the hulls of 3 lemons and 8 sprigs of mint. Remove from heat and let steep 10 minutes. Add 2 cups sugar and stir to dissolve. Strain into a 1-gallon jar and add water to fill gallon. Chill and serve over ice.

Basket Barbeque

BARBEQUED HAMBURGERS

These hamburgers have a different and delicious flavor. The secret is the special no-cook sauce. Make six patties from 1½ lbs. of ground meat the day before the party. Place in bowl and cover with Basket Barbeque Sauce. Cover and refrigerate 24 hours. Broil 10–15 minutes, turning once. Baste with sauce. Serve with onion slices.

BASKET BARBEQUE SAUCE

½ cup salad oil	1 teaspoon lemon juice
½ cup chili sauce	2 lemon slices
1 cup vinegar	1 teaspoon Worcestershire
1 tablespoon chopped onion	½ teaspoon chili powder
1 clove garlic	¼ cup brown sugar

Combine all ingredients and mix well—no need to cook!

SATURDAY NIGHT SPECIAL BEANS

1 cup Navy or pea beans	1 tablespoon dry mustard
1 cup lima beans	½ teaspoon ginger
1 cup kidney beans	½ teaspoon pepper
1 cup yellow-eye beans	½ cup brown sugar
2 teaspoons salt	½ cup molasses or maple syrup
½ lb. salt pork	1 tablespoon Worcestershire
2 small onions, chopped	

Sort and wash all dry beans. Soak overnight in water to cover. Add salt and additional water to cover well. Bring slowly to boil. Simmer until skins of beans wrinkle. Drain. Save liquid. Put a ¼-inch slice of pork in bottom of deep pot (an old fashioned bean pot is best, but a covered casserole will do). Alternate layers of beans with sprinkling of chopped onion until pot is two-thirds full. Score remainder of pork through the rind in ½-inch squares, ½-inch deep. Bury pork in top of beans with only rind exposed. Heat liquid from drained beans and add remaining ingredients. Pour all over beans, adding extra boiling water to top level of beans. Cover. Bake at 225 degrees 6–7 hours. Uncover last hour. Add more water if needed. Serves 8–10. Best scratch beans ever!

BEST CANNED BAKED BEANS

Canned pork 'n beans
Onions

Bacon
Molasses

People always remark at the tastiness of these beans. Drain canned baked beans and then layer in a casserole: beans, thinly sliced onion rings, bacon and covering of molasses. Layer again as much as you need. Cook at least 6 hours at 250 degrees or longer if you have a large amount of beans.

MOIST HAMBURGER BUNS

Butter buns and wrap each one separately in waxed paper. Heat in a preheated 200-degree oven for 20 minutes Serve steamy buns with Barbequed Hamburgers *and a platter of hamburger dress-ups: lettuce, sliced tomatoes, sliced onions, hamburger dills, relish, creole or* Spicy Mustard *and* Blender Mayonnaise.

PEACH ICE CREAM

3 eggs
1 tablespoon flour or cornstarch
1 quart sweet milk
1 (15-oz.) can condensed milk

1 tablespoon vanilla
3 cups mashed peaches, sweetened
to taste with sugar

Beat eggs. Add flour dissolved in a little milk, add milk, and cook in double boiler or over slow heat till it coats the spoon. Remove from heat and cool. Add condensed milk, vanilla and peaches. Freeze in ice cream freezer. This ice cream is delicious even without the peaches. Or substitute strawberries, if desired. Makes about 2 quarts.

BUTTERMILK POUND CAKE

2 sticks margarine, softened
2½ cups sugar
5 eggs, separated
3 cups flour

¼ teaspoon salt
1 cup buttermilk
½ teaspoon soda
2 teaspoons vanilla

Cream margarine. Add sugar gradually, then egg yolks, one at a time, beating after each addition. Dissolve soda in buttermilk. Add flour alternately with milk, starting and ending with flour. Add vanilla. Beat egg whites until stiff; fold in. Bake in a greased and floured tube pan at 300 degrees for 45 minutes. Serves 24.

SEPTEMBER

THE MOOD IS GREEK

The beautiful blue Mediterranean provided the inspiration for the blue and white Greek flag. Bands of blue ribbon down a white tablecloth along with blue candles provide an appealing background for your Grecian delicacies. Place grapes around candlesticks. Serve the salad on purple cabbage leaves.

Kotopits (Chicken in Filo)
Grecian Salad
Baked Tomatoes Rockefeller
Mt. Olympus Dill Bread
Parthenon Chocolate Pie
Greek Gingerale

SATURDAY NIGHT SUPPER CLUB

This is the time to get back into the swing of things. Get the supper club together for a relaxed meal. After this hearty supper, serve pick-up desserts while mutual friends are mingling and catching up on the news.

Jon Marzette
Hodge-Podge Salad
California Vegetable Marinade
Buttery Soft French Bread
Keepsake Brownies or
Irresistible Chess Squares

The Mood is Greek

KOTOPITS
(CHICKEN IN FILO)

8 oz. frozen filo dough	½ teaspoon salt
1 cup chopped celery	½ teaspoon nutmeg
¾ cup chopped onion	Few dashes pepper
1 tablespoon butter	1 beaten egg
2½ cups chopped cooked chicken	6 tablespoons butter, melted
2 tablespoons chicken broth	Hot cooked rice
2 teaspoons dried parsley flakes	Bechamel Sauce

Thaw filo dough (10–12 sheets) at room temperature. In large covered skillet, cook celery and onion in butter till tender but not brown. Add chicken and broth. Cook and stir, uncovered, till all broth is absorbed. Set aside. For each roll, stack half (5–6 sheets) of filo dough, brushing generously with melted butter between each layer. Spoon half of chicken mixture over filo layers to within 1 inch of edges. Turn 1 short side over filling about 1 inch; fold in long sides. Roll as for jelly roll starting with folded short side. Place seam side down on a lightly greased baking pan. Repeat with remaining filo and filling. Brush each roll with additional melted butter. Score each roll into 3 or 4 portions. Bake in 350-degree oven 40 minutes or until rolls are brown and crisp. Cut rolls where scored. Arrange on platter with hot cooked rice. Spoon some Bechamel Sauce *over rolls. Pass remaining sauce. Serves 6–8.*

BECHAMEL SAUCE

2 tablespoons butter	1¼ cups chicken broth
2 tablespoons flour	2 beaten egg yolks
½ teaspoon salt	4 teaspoons lemon juice

Melt butter in saucepan; stir in flour and salt. Add broth all at once. Cook and stir until mixture is bubbly. Combine egg yolks and lemon juice. Stir about half the hot mixture into egg yolk mixture. Return to remaining hot mixture in pan. Cook and stir 2 minutes more.

GRECIAN SALAD

½ cup olive oil
½ cup lemon juice
¼ teaspoon pepper
1 medium head lettuce
1 cucumber, pared

10 cherry tomatoes or 2 large
tomatoes, cut into wedges
½ cup calamata (Greek-style) or
ripe olives
4 oz. feta cheese, cubed

Combine olive oil, lemon juice and pepper and set aside. Tear lettuce into small pieces in a wooden salad bowl. Cut cucumbers into chunks and toss gently with lettuce and dressing. Garnish with olives, tomatoes and cheese. Serves 6.

BAKED TOMATOES ROCKEFELLER

12 thick slices of tomatoes
2 (10-oz.) pkgs. frozen, chopped
spinach
1 cup seasoned bread crumbs
6 chopped green onions
2 eggs, slightly beaten
1 stick butter, melted
¼ cup Parmesan cheese

1 teaspoon Worcestershire
2 cloves garlic, minced
1 teaspoon salt
½ teaspoon pepper
¾ teaspoon thyme
1 teaspoon Accent
2 teaspoons lemon juice
Several drops Tabasco

Cook spinach according to directions and drain well. Add remaining ingredients except tomato slices. Arrange tomatoes in a single layer in a buttered baking dish. Top slices with spinach mixture. Bake at 350 degrees about 15 minutes. Serves 12.

MT. OLYMPUS DILL BREAD

1 envelope yeast, softened in
¼ cup warm water
1 cup creamed cottage cheese
3 tablespoons butter
2 tablespoons sugar
1 tablespoon instant dry onion

2 teaspoons dill seed
1 teaspoon salt
¼ teaspoon baking soda
1 egg, unbeaten
2¼–2½ cups plain flour

Heat cottage cheese and butter to lukewarm. Combine all ingredients except flour in large bowl. Mix, adding flour gradually to form a stiff dough. Cover and let rise 50–60 minutes in warm place. Then stir down and turn into a well-greased large bowl. When doubled, put dough in 3 loaf pans. Let rise 30–40 minutes until again doubled. Bake in 350-degree oven 40–50 minutes or until golden. Easy to double.

GREEK GINGERALE

1 (6-oz.) can frozen lemonade
1 (46-oz.) can grapefruit juice

1 (46-oz.) can pineapple juice
1 quart gingerale

Mix all together and chill. Serve over ice in tall glasses. Makes 3 quarts.

PARTHENON CHOCOLATE PIE

½ stick butter, melted
1½ cups sugar
3 tablespoons cocoa
2 eggs

Dash of salt
1 small can evaporated milk
1 teaspoon vanilla
1 unbaked pie shell

Mix all ingredients and pour into unbaked pie shell. Bake 35 minutes at 325 degrees. Serve with scoop of ice cream or whipped cream.

Saturday Night Supper Club

JON MARZETTE

1 lb. ground beef
1 lb. ground pork
2 large onions, chopped
2 large green peppers, chopped
5 stalks celery, chopped
1 can tomato soup
1 (6-oz.) can mushroom stems
and pieces
1 (12-oz.) can tomato juice
¼ teaspoon oregano
¼ teaspoon thyme
15–20 green olives, sliced

1 can water with liquid from
mushrooms
1 teaspoon sugar
1 (1-lb.) can spaghetti sauce
1 teaspoon salt
1 teaspoon pepper
2 teaspoons Worcestershire
½ lb. grated sharp cheese
1 (16-oz.) pkg. wide noodles,
cooked and drained
Buttered bread crumbs

Brown meats together with onions, green peppers and celery—do not brown too much. Add all other ingredients except cheese, bread crumbs and noodles. Simmer for about 1 hour. Add half the cheese, then combine with cooked, drained noodles. Put in two, 2-quart buttered casseroles. Top with the remaining cheese and buttered bread crumbs. Refrigerate, freeze or bake immediately 25–30 minutes in 375-degree oven. Serves 10–12.

HODGE-PODGE SALAD

Use 3 different kinds of lettuce, washed and torn into bite-sized pieces. Toss lightly with an oil and vinegar dressing and top with croutons and a sliced hardcooked egg.

CALIFORNIA VEGETABLE MARINADE

Hearts of palm, drained
Artichokes, drained

Fresh tomatoes, cut in chunks
Green pepper, cut bite-sized

Marinate all ingredients in Wishbone Italian dressing overnight. Serve with slotted spoon.

BUTTERY SOFT FRENCH BREAD

Add ½ teaspoon garlic salt to ½ cup melted butter. Spoon over 2 split halves of a loaf of French bread. Wrap tightly in foil and bake at least 15 minutes in 375-degree oven—or along with Jon Marzette.

KEEPSAKE BROWNIES

This recipe has been a treasured keepsake for many years. They are so rich they are almost like candy, so moist they keep well—if there are any left to keep!

4 squares unsweetened chocolate
1 cup butter
2 cups sugar
3 eggs, beaten

1 teaspoon vanilla
1 cup chopped pecans
1 cup sifted, plain flour
¼ teaspoon salt

Melt chocolate and butter over hot water. Remove from heat. Add sugar, eggs and vanilla. Mix well. Stir in pecans. Sift flour and salt together and gradually mix in, beating entire mixture well. Pour into greased and floured 9" square pan. Bake in 350-degree oven 45—50 minutes. Cool before cutting into squares.

IRRESISTIBLE CHESS SQUARES

1 box butter cake mix
1 egg
1 stick butter, melted
3 additional eggs

1 (8-oz.) pkg. cream cheese, softened
1 (1-lb.) box powdered sugar
2 teaspoons vanilla

Mix first 3 ingredients well and spread with a small spatula in a 9 x 13" baking dish. Blend next four ingredients well and pour on top of cake mixture. Be sure to spread evenly. Bake at 350 degrees 30—40 minutes. Cool and cut into squares. Similar to chess pie in taste and texture.

OCTOBER

MEXICAN FIESTA

The inspiration for this party comes from our southern neighbors. Use a serape as a runner for your table. Arrange flowers in Mexican pottery, using red, white, green and yellow—the colors of the Mexican flag. Hang a piñata for after dinner entertainment.

Natchos
Tamale Delights.
Avocado-Grapefruit Salad
Beefy Mexican Cornbread
Mexi-Beans
Orange-Lemon Ice Cream
Cinnamon Siesta Tea

FOOTBALL KICKOFF BRUNCH

What better way to serve your Delta dove than at a football brunch! The enthusiam of the fans before the game is always upbeat. Entice your guests by printing the menu on your invitations. Football-shaped name tags save all from embarrassment!

Delicious Delta Dove
Gridiron Grits
Touchdown Tomatoes
Fruit Compote
Pass Around Biscuits

Lemon Muffins
Green Tomato Pickle
Champion Chocolate Cake or
Prune Bundt Cake
Football Jug Punch

Mexican Fiesta

NATCHOS

Cut sliced sharp Cheddar cheese to fit Doritos or Tostitos. Then seed and slice whole green chilis (canned) into bite-sized pieces. Layer cheese and chilis on chips on cookie sheet. Bake in 350-degree oven until cheese is melted. Serve hot.

TAMALE DELIGHTS

Cut 6 tamales into bite-sized pieces. Wrap each piece with ½ slice of bacon. Broil until bacon is crisp, turning frequently. Serve hot.

BEEFY MEXICAN CORNBREAD

¾ lb. ground beef
1 large onion, chopped
½ lb. Cheddar cheese, grated
1 cup yellow cornmeal
½ teaspoon soda

1 cup milk
½ cup bacon grease, melted
1 (No. 2) can yellow cream corn
½ teaspoon salt
4 finely chopped Jalapeno peppers

Brown meat with onion. Grate cheese and set aside. Combine cornmeal, soda, milk, bacon grease, corn, salt and Jalapeno peppers. Heat a large greased skillet; sprinkle cornmeal over bottom. Pour in half the batter; put meat layer on top of this. Sprinkle cheese over meat and top with remaining batter. Cook in 350-degree oven 45–50 minutes. Serves 6.

AVOCADO-GRAPEFRUIT SALAD

Ripe avocado
Fresh or canned grapefruit sections

Lettuce
Wishbone French dressing

Slice avocado into long slices. Arrange attractively on lettuce cup with grapefruit sections. Top with French dressing. The secret to this salad is a perfectly ripe avocado. Buy a firm one 3 or 4 days prior to the day you need it and let it ripen at home.

MEXI-BEANS

4 slices bacon, diced
½ medium onion, chopped
2 (1-lb.) cans Pinto, beans, drained

½ teaspoon ground cumin seed
½ teaspoon coriander
1 clove garlic, pressed
½ teaspoon salt

Fry bacon until almost done; add onions and continue cooking till onions are slightly browned and bacon is crisp. Add beans and seasonings and heat slowly. Serve with bottled Picante Sauce. Serves 6.

ORANGE-LEMON ICE CREAM

This is very easy and really delicious—perfect after a Mexican meal!

1 (12-oz.) can frozen orange juice
1 (6-oz.) can frozen lemonade
2 (½-pt.) cartons whipping cream

2 cups sugar
5 cups milk

Mix all ingredients together and stir well. Freeze in ice cream freezer. Makes 2 quarts.

CINNAMON SIESTA TEA

12 cups water
1 teaspoon whole cloves
1 teaspoon whole allspice
1 stick cinnamon

4 teabags
1 (6-oz.) can frozen orange juice
1 (6-oz.) can frozen lemonade
1 (46-oz.) can pineapple juice

Boil water. Add spices. Simmer 5 minutes. Add tea bags and let sit for one hour. Add sugar and juices. Refrigerate. Serve hot or cold.

Football Kickoff Brunch

DELICIOUS DELTA DOVE

15 dove
Salt and pepper
Flour
½ cup salad oil

1 cup Worcestershire
1 cup red wine
1 cup water
Juice of 2 lemons

Salt, pepper and flour the dove and brown in oil. Pour grease off and add remaining ingredients. In a pan with a tight-fitting lid, cook on top of stove slowly or in oven at 325 degrees for 2–3 hours. Can be cooked in crockpot for 8 to 10 hours.

GRIDIRON GRITS

1 cup uncooked grits (not instant)
4 cups water
1 stick butter or margarine

1 (6-oz.) pkg. garlic cheese
2 eggs
Sweet milk as needed
Seasoned salt

Cook grits in water according to package directions. Add butter and cheese. Beat eggs in a cup and add milk to make 1 cup full. Season well with seasoned salt. Cook 1 hour (or until middle of casserole does not wiggle) in 300-degree oven. Serves 8.

TOUCHDOWN TOMATOES

2 (1-lb.) cans whole tomatoes
2 tablespoons brown sugar
2 teaspoons salt
½ teaspoon dried chervil

½ teaspoon seasoned salt
2 tablespoons chopped chives
4 grinds fresh black pepper
Course dry bread crumbs

Put tomatoes with juice in open casserole. Mix in all other ingredients except bread crumbs. Scatter crumbs on top and bake at 250 degrees for 2 hours. Really delicious with almost anything! Serves 6.

FRUIT COMPOTE

1 large can fruit for salads
1 can pears
1 can pineapple chunks
1 can apricots

Fresh grapefruit sections
Fresh orange sections
Mayonnaise
Sour cream

Drain all canned fruit for at least an hour. Add fresh grapefruit sections and fresh orange sections to canned fruit. Mix equal amounts of mayonnaise and sour cream and toss lightly until coated. Serve in a glass bowl.

PASS AROUND BISCUITS

2 cups sifted flour
5 tablespoons shortening
1 teaspoon salt

3 teaspoons baking powder
¾ cup sweet milk

Cut shortening in flour. Add salt, baking powder and milk. Shape dough down and knead it eight times. Don't roll—press dough out. Cut with cookie cutter and prick with fork. Place on greased cookie sheet and bake at 450 degrees 10—12 minutes. Makes 16 biscuits.

LEMON MUFFINS

½ cup margarine
½ cup sugar
1 tablespoon grated lemon rind
2 eggs, separated
1 cup flour
1 teaspoon baking powder

¼ teaspoon salt
3 tablespoons lemon juice
1 tablespoon additional sugar
1 teaspoon nutmeg
¼ cup chopped pecans

Cream margarine. Gradually add sugar and lemon rind, beating until light and fluffy. Add egg yolks one at a time, mixing well after each. Sift together flour, baking powder and salt. Add flour mixture alternately with lemon juice. Beat egg whites until stiff peaks form. Fold egg whites into batter; spoon into 12 greased 2½" muffin cups or 36 tiny tart cups. Bake at 375 degrees 20—25 minutes for large or at 350 degrees 15—20 minutes for small tins.

GREEN TOMATO PICKLE

1 gallon cold water
½ cup lime
7 lbs. sliced green tomatoes
2 qts. vinegar

5 lbs. sugar
1 tablespoon whole cloves
1 tablespoon whole allspice
1 tablespoon whole cinnamon

Put lime in water to cover sliced tomatoes and soak overnight (or 10—12 hours). Lift tomatoes out of water carefully so as not to break them. Wash carefully to get the lime off. Put vinegar and sugar in large pot to boil. Put spices in a bag. When sugar and vinegar begin to boil, add tomatoes and spice bag. Cook slowly until tomatoes are clear— about 2—2½ hours. Put these up in self-sealing jars. These make nice Christmas presents. Tastes good with all kinds of meat and fowl.

FOOTBALL JUG PUNCH

In a 1-gallon plastic container (jug), mix together 2 (6-oz.) cans frozen orange juice, 2 (6-oz.) cans frozen lemonade, 1 (46-oz.) can pineapple juice and 1 cup sugar. Fill the rest of the jug with water. Freeze. Three hours before serving, remove from freezer. Punch will be mushy. At serving time, pour into punch bowl and add 2 quarts Sprite. Serves 40.

CHAMPION CHOCOLATE CAKE

1 stick butter
1 stick oleo
1 cup water
4 tablespoons cocoa
2 cups sugar
1 teaspoon soda

2 cups plus 2 tablespoons cake
flour or 2 cups all-purpose
flour
2 eggs
½ cup buttermilk
1 teaspoon vanilla

Melt first 4 ingredients over low heat. Sift dry ingredients together. Combine the 2 mixtures then add eggs, buttermilk and vanilla. Bake in greased and floured 9 x 12 x 1½" pan in preheated 350-degree oven for 45 mintues or until done.

CHAMPION FROSTING

½ stick oleo
3 tablespoons buttermilk

1½ tablespoons cocoa
½ box powdered sugar, sifted

Melt first 3 ingredients. Beat in powdered sugar, adding more if necessary. Add ½ teaspoon vanilla, if desired. Ice cake while still in pan. Cut into squares to serve.

PRUNE BUNDT CAKE

2 cups self-rising flour
2 cups sugar
1 teaspoon cinnamon
1 teaspoon allspice
1 teaspoon nutmeg

3 eggs
1 cup corn oil
2 babyfood jars prunes with
tapioca
1 teaspoon vanilla

Mix all together well. Bake at 350 degrees in greased, floured bundt pan for 45–55 minutes. Frost with Caramel Icing.

CARAMEL ICING

2½ cups sugar
½ pt. whipping cream

1 stick butter
2 teaspoons vanilla

Bring 2 cups sugar, cream, butter almost to a boil. Carmalize remaining ½ cup sugar and add to first mixture. Bring to a soft-ball stage. Cool. Add vanilla. Beat with mixer until spreading consistency. Ice cake.

NOVEMBER

ELECTION NIGHT DINNER

Listening to the election returns, whether local, state or national, always prompts good food, fun and fellowship. Agreement is not a prerequisite for an invitation. Have several TV sets around for easy viewing.

Victory Pork Roast
Ballot Box Bread Sticks
Down Home Turnip Greens
Candidates' Sweet Potatoes
Senator's Squash Casserole
Winning Apple Cake

BOUNTIFUL BLESSINGS

We have such a wonderfully rich heritage of tradition for Thanksgiving. Create a striking centerpiece by using a wooden duck decoy placed on green styrofoam covered with Spanish moss, magnolia leaves and all kinds of fresh fruit—an easy task if you live in the Deep South!

Traditional Turkey with Giblet Gravy
Gobbler's Cornbread Dressing
Harvest Fruit Salad
Sweet Potatoes in Orange Cups
Pilgrim's Peas With Water Chestnuts
Bountiful Rolls
Ambrosia Cake

Election Night Dinner

VICTORY PORK ROAST

1 (4–5 lb.) boned, rolled and tied pork loin roast	2 cloves garlic, minced
½ cup soy sauce	1 tablespoon dry mustard
½ cup dry sherry	1 teaspoon ginger
	1 teaspoon thyme, crushed

Marinate loin roast at room temperature for 2–3 hours or overnight in refrigerator in mixture of all other ingredients. Roast, uncovered, at 325 degrees for 2½–3 hours, basting every 30 minutes with marinade. Serves 6–8.

BALLOT BOX BREAD STICKS

1 cup cornmeal	¾ cup milk
½ cup flour	1 egg, beaten
3 teaspoons baking powder	3 tablespoons vegetable shorten-
½ teaspoon salt	ing or bacon grease, melted

Combine all dry ingredients. Add milk, egg and shortening. Beat until fairly smooth, about 1 minute. Bake in greased cornbread stick pan or muffin tins in 425-degree oven for 15–20 minutes.

DOWN HOME TURNIP GREENS

Wash turnip greens thoroughly. Pick off leaves and take out the tough stems. Put sliced salt meat in water with some sugar and boil about 20 minutes. Add turnip greens and some turnips. Add some bacon grease and cook slowly until tender. Season with salt, pepper and seasoned salt. The secret to cooking fresh vegetables is in the seasoning—you must taste as you cook. Serve pepper vinegar along with turnip greens.

CANDIDATES' SWEET POTATOES

6 medium sweet potatoes	½ cup butter, melted
1 orange, thickly sliced, with peel	1½ cups sugar
	1½ cups light Karo syrup

Peel potatoes and cover with water. Bring to a boil and add orange slices. Cook until almost tender. Arrange potatoes in 1½-quart baking dish. Add Karo and sugar to melted butter and mix well. Pour syrup over potatoes and let stand in refrigerator overnight. Cook slowly, 250 degrees, covered for 1 hour. Uncover and continue cooking for 1 more hour. Serves 6.

SENATOR'S SQUASH CASSEROLE

1 medium onion, chopped	1½ cups grated sharp cheese
1 stick butter, melted	Salt and pepper to taste
10 medium yellow squash	1 can cream of chicken soup
1 teaspoon sugar	7 crackers, crushed
2 eggs, beaten	

Saute onion in stick of butter until tender. Cook squash with sugar, drain and mash. Mix all ingredients together except cracker crumbs, then pour into greased 3-qt. casserole dish. Top with cracker crumbs. Cook at 325 degrees for 45 minutes. Serves 8–10.

WINNING APPLE CAKE

4 apples, thinly sliced	2 teaspoons baking powder
2 cups sugar	4 teaspoons cinnamon
3 eggs	2½ cups all purpose flour
1¼ cups cooking oil	1 teaspoon vanilla
1 teaspoon soda	1 cup chopped pecans
1 teaspoon salt	

Core, peel and thinly slice 4 large apples. Mix together sugar and eggs. Add oil and beat 1 minute. Sift together soda, salt, baking powder, cinnamon and flour. Fold dry ingredients into liquid. Add vanilla and pecans. Lastly, fold in apples. Put into a 13 x 8" pan and bake at 325 degrees for 1 hour. Top with the following sauce:

WINNING SAUCE

1 cup sugar	½ cup evaporated milk
1 stick butter	1 teaspoon vanilla

Cook first 3 ingredients 1 minute, stirring constantly. Add vanilla. Pour hot sauce over cake. Extra delicious to garnish with a dollop of whipped cream. Serves 10.

TRADITIONAL TURKEY

Wash turkey and pat dry. Salt outside of turkey well. Rub generously with oleo and stuff lightly. Place in regular turkey cooker or shallow pan on rack. Put double layer of cheese cloth soaked in salad oil over bird. Soak 3 or 4 times during cooking. Put aluminum foil over just the breast until ready to brown bird. Place bird straight from refrigerator to a 450-degree preheated oven. Reduce heat immediately to 325 degrees. Cook bird to an internal temperature of 180–185 degrees. Center of stuffing should reach 165 degrees. A turkey should rest about 20 minutes after removal from oven before carving. Serve with homemade or canned cranberry sauce.

GIBLET GRAVY

¼ cup fat drippings from cooked turkey
¼ cup flour
2–3 cups turkey broth

2 celery tops
3 lemon slices
Neck, liver, gizzard from turkey
Salt, pepper, seasoned salt

Cook neck, liver, gizzard in water which has been seasoned with lemon slices, celery tops, salt and pepper until tender. Pull meat off neck bone and chop with other meats very small. Strain broth and reserve in refrigerator until you make gravy. This may be done a day ahead of time. (Cover it well.) To make gravy, mix fat and flour in skillet and stir until golden brown. Add chicken broth until of gravy consistency. Season well! Add chopped meat to gravy, heat and serve.

GOBBLER'S CORNBREAD DRESSING

1 cup turkey broth
½ cup oleo
1 cup diced celery
1 cup diced onion
1 skillet of cornbread
2 teaspoons or more of salt

Scant ¼ teaspoon baking powder
½ teaspoon or more pepper
Poultry seasoning to taste (start with
 ½–1 teaspoon)
3 or 4 beaten eggs
1 box Kellogg's croutons

To make turkey broth, place in saucepan turkey neck, liver and gizzard and add enough water to cover generously. Add salt, red pepper, sliced lemon, celery stalk and boil until meat is tender. Add the liver a little later, as it cooks quicker.

To make dressing, soak 6 slices of bread in pan of water. Squeeze out excess water. Saute celery and onions in oleo until tender. Combine with crumbled cornbread, bread, seasonings, eggs and ½ box croutons. Sprinkle broth over dressing and mix lightly. You may add more of the croutons and more broth to keep it from being too dry or too moist. If you choose not to use croutons, increase amount of cornbread.

HARVEST FRUIT SALAD

1 (8-oz.) carton whipped topping
4 oz. cream cheese, softened
1 large can crushed pineapple
½ cup nuts, coarsely chopped

1 jar Ocean Spray cranberry relish
1 (8-oz.) can Mandarin oranges
1½ cups miniature marshmallows
Mayonnaise

Cream topping and cream cheese and add drained fruit and nuts, folding to mix well. Pour into 9 x 12" casserole or mold. Serve on large tray with lettuce and mayonnaise. Serves 8.

SWEET POTATOES IN ORANGE CUPS

6 oranges, halved
6 tablespoons butter
3 tablespoons orange juice
2 tablespoons sugar

½ teaspoon salt
¼ teaspoon nutmeg
6 yams, cooked, peeled and
 mashed

Remove orange pieces from halves and set aside. Squeeze pieces in a bowl to get 3 tablespoons orange juice. In a small saucepan, combine butter, juice, sugar, salt and nutmeg. Simmer mixture for three minutes, stirring often. Pour mixture over mashed yams. Beat until fluffy. Spoon mixture into orange cups. Bake at 350 degrees for 30 mintues. Serves 6.

PILGRIM'S PEAS WITH WATER CHESTNUTS

2 (16-oz.) cans LeSueur peas
1 can sliced water chestnuts

½ stick butter
Salt and pepper

Heat peas and water chestnuts in liquid. Drain most of liquid. Add butter and seasonings.

BOUNTIFUL ROLLS

1 cup milk
1 cup hot water
3 pkgs. yeast
1 tablespoon salt

½–¾ cup sugar
2 eggs, beaten
6 cups flour
½ cup vegetable oil

Combine milk and hot water. Dissolve yeast in this mixture and mix well. Add salt, sugar, and eggs. Mix 3 cups flour into milk mixture. Add oil. Mix in remainding 3 cups flour. Cover and let rise in warm place till doubled. Punch down and refrigerate or roll out into rolls immediately. Bake at 400 degrees until done, about 10–15 minutes.

AMBROSIA CAKE

2 cups sugar
½ cup butter
1 square unsweetened chocolate
½ cup boiling water
3 eggs, beaten separately

2 teaspoons soda
½ teaspoon cinnamon
1 teaspoon ground cloves
½ teaspoon nutmeg

Cream sugar and butter. Dissolve chocolate in boiling water and add to creamed mixture. Add beaten egg yolks and spices. Then add flour alternately with milk. Beat egg whites till stiff and fold into mixture. Put in 3 greased 9" cake pans. Bake at 375 degrees 30–40 minutes.

AMBROSIA FILLING

3 cups sugar
2 cups evaporated milk
Pinch of soda
1 teaspoon baking powder
1 tablespoon butter

1 cup grated coconut
1 cup raisins
1 cup pecans, chopped
1 grated orange rind

Cook sugar with milk until thickened. Remove from heat, add remaining ingredients (including some cut-up orange pulp) and mix well. Spread between layers of cake and on top.

DECEMBER

HOLIDAY OPEN HOUSE

Christmastime is the time to spread "good will towards men." Open your heart and your home to family and friends. Plan ahead and utilize your freezer. It's important to arrange your trays attractively and garnish well. Avoid congestion in the dining room by serving sweets and coffee in another room.

Carved Smoked Turkey
Smoked Brisket with Sauce
Spicy Mustard
Blender Mayonnaise
Shrimp Mold
Tomato Aspic Canapes
Warm Christmas Wassail

Cheese Wreath
Vegetable Platter
Festive Broccoli Dip
Toasted Pecans
Santa's Shortbread Cookies
Jingle Bell Squares
Butter Pecan Turtle Cookies

CHRISTMASTIME BRUNCH

Holidays are wonderful times for getting out of the routine. Let's skip breakfast and begin with that in-between gathering called brunch. Plan ahead, fix ahead, even set your table ahead—a fun occasion!

Grillades with Grits or Rice
Dixie Oysters
Hot Curried Fruit
Zippy Spinach Madeleine
Store-Some-More Biscuits
Southern Pecan Pie

Holiday Open House

CARVED SMOKED TURKEY

Salt turkey heavily all over outside and inside breast cavity. Place bird in large paper bag and refrigerate 24 hours. Before smoking, rinse salt off of turkey and dry well with paper towels. Sprinkle with lemon-pepper marinade and rub heavily with peanut oil. Smoke turkey on grill for 6–8 hours. Carve thinly for sandwiches.

SMOKED BRISKET WITH SAUCE

1 tablespoon liquid smoke
1½ tablespoons brown sugar
½ cup catsup
¼ cup water
1 teaspoon celery seed

3 tablespoons melted butter
2 tablespoons Worcestershire
1½ teaspoons dry mustard
Dash of pepper

Combine all ingredients in saucepan and simmer 5 minutes. Marinate brisket in sauce overnight in refrigerator. Cook brisket in smoker about 12 hours, basting as you can. Chill brisket and then slice very thinly.

SPICY MUSTARD

1 cup brown sugar
1 tablespoon flour
1 (2-oz.) can dry mustard
½ teaspoon salt

½ cup vinegar
½ cup water
3 egg yolks
1 bouillon cube

Mix dry ingredients in saucepan and add liquid. Add egg yolks and bouillon cube. Cook and stir 10 minutes. Refrigerate in a jar.

BLENDER MAYONNAISE

2 large eggs
1½ teaspoons salt
½ teaspoon dry mustard
Pinch of white pepper

¼ teaspoon paprika
2 tablespoons fresh lemon juice
1 cup salad oil

Place all ingredients except oil in blender jar. Blend at high speed about 10 seconds, then add oil in a thin, steady stream. Run blender another minute. Occasionally stop to scrape sides of blender. Makes 1¼ cups.

SHRIMP MOLD

2 envelopes unflavored gelatin
11 oz. of cream cheese
3 tablespoons mayonnaise
1½ tablespoons lemon juice
1 teaspoon Tabasco
Few drops red food coloring
Salt and pepper to taste

1 lb. shrimp, cooked and de-
veined, shelled, finely chopped
½ cup celery, finely chopped
1 onion, grated
1 green pepper, finely chopped
2 hardcooked eggs, chopped

Dissolve gelatin in 2 tablespoons cold water and just enough hot water to melt. Mix with next 5 ingredients. Add remaining ingredients and put in greased fish or Jello mold. Chill until firm. Unmold and serve with crackers. Superb!

TOMATO ASPIC CANAPES

2 cups tomato juice
¼ cup finely chopped celery
¼ cup finely chopped onion
Juice of 1 lemon
2 tablespoons Worcestershire

Dash of Tabasco
Salt and pepper to taste
2 envelopes plain gelatin
¼ cup cold water
Ritz crackers

Boil and simmer first 3 ingredients 5 minutes. Remove from heat and add lemon juice, Worcestershire, Tabasco, salt and pepper. Then dissolve gelatin in water. Strain the tomato juice mixture and add softened gelatin. Place in greased 9 x 12" Pyrex dish. Refrigerate until firm. Cut aspic into desired shape to fit Ritz crackers. Serve with dollop of mayonnaise and a sliced olive on top. These keep well on buffet table. Makes about 35.

WARM CHRISTMAS WASSAIL

2 quarts apple cider
3 cinnamon sticks
2 teaspoons nutmeg

2 teaspoons cloves
½ cup fresh lemon juice
2 cups fresh orange juice

Boil cider and spices together 15 minutes. Add juices and simmer. Serve warm in mugs. Makes 10 servings.

CHEESE WREATH

1 cup chopped pecans
½ cup chopped parsley
1 lb. Velveeta cheese

1 (8-oz.) pkg. cream cheese
¼ lb. Roquefort cheese
½ cup chopped green onions

Reserve ¼ cup parsley. Bring cheeses to room temperature and blend all ingredients. Roll and shape into wreath and chill. Press parsley into surface of wreath. Pretty to garnish with bow or holly at top or center.

VEGETABLE PLATTER WITH CURRY DIP

½ cup mayonnaise
1 cup sour cream
2 tablespoons lemon juice
Salt and pepper to taste
1 teaspoon curry powder
½ teaspoon paprika

2 tablespoons minced parsley
½ teaspoon dried crushed tarragon
2 tablespoons grated onion
2 teaspoons prepared mustard
1 tablespoon minced chives
5 dashes Tabasco

Combine mayonnaise, sour cream and lemon juice. Blend with all other ingredients and chill overnight before serving. Makes about 1¾ cups. Use as a dip for an assortment of raw vegetables such as: yellow squash slices, carrot, cucumber and celery sticks, and cauliflower and broccoli flowerettes.

FESTIVE BROCCOLI DIP

1 stick margarine
1 large onion, chopped
2 pkgs. frozen chopped broccoli
1 roll garlic cheese

1 can mushroom soup
1 small can mushrooms, sliced
1 cup bread crumbs
Salt and pepper to taste

Melt margarine in large skillet. Add onion and broccoli. Cook about 30 minutes. Add cheese and soup and stir until cheese is melted. Add mushrooms and bread crumbs. Season. Serve in chafing dish with Melba rounds. Enough for party of 16.

TOASTED PECANS

2 cups pecan halves

1 stick real butter

Heat oven to 250 degrees. Place pecan halves on cookie sheet. Put chunks of real butter on cookie sheet with pecans. Place in oven and stir pecans about every 5 minutes, making sure butter coats all pecans. Watch carefully so they do not burn. When they are nicely brown, place pecans on a paper towel to drain. Salt to taste. These will keep in a covered tin for months.

SANTA'S SHORTBREAD COOKIES

1 lb. real butter (do not sub-
    stitute)

2 cups sugar
6 cups flour

Cream butter and sugar until light yellow. Sift flour into butter-sugar mixture. Knead with hands. Roll into 3 long rolls, wrap in waxed paper and refrigerate. When cold, slice as thinly as possible and put on a cookie sheet. Decorate with red and green sugar sprinkles, if desired. Bake at 325 degrees 15 minutes or until light brown. Yields 6 dozen.

JINGLE BELL SQUARES

2 cups vanilla wafers, crushed
1 stick oleo, melted
1 (6-oz.) pkg. chocolate chips

1 cup canned coconut
1 cup chopped pecans
1 can condensed milk

Line bottom of pan with vanilla wafer crumbs and melted oleo. Layer in this order: chocolate chips, coconut, pecans, and pour condensed milk over all. Bake 30 minutes at 350 degrees. Cool and cut into tiny squares.

BUTTER PECAN TURTLE COOKIES

This recipe is a must to make. It came all the way from Maine to our kitchen way down South.

2 cups flour
1 cup brown sugar
½ cup butter, softened
1 cup whole pecan halves

1 stick plus 3 tablespoons butter
½ cup brown sugar
1 cup milk chocolate chips

In large bowl, combine flour, brown sugar and butter. Mix until very fine and pat firmly into a 9 x 13 x 2" pan. Sprinkle pecans evenly over unbaked crust. In a heavy saucepan, combine brown sugar and butter. Cook over medium heat, stirring constantly, until surface of mixture begins to boil. Boil 1 minute, stirring constantly. Pour caramel layer evenly over pecans and crust. Bake near center of 350-degree oven for 18–22 minutes or until entire layer is bubbly and crust is light golden. Remove from oven and immediately sprinkle with milk chocolate chips. Allow chips to begin to melt, 2–3 minutes. Slightly swirl chips as they melt, leaving some whole for marbled effect. Do not spread chips. Cool completely before cutting into squares.

Christmastime Brunch

GRILLADES

Creole grillades ("gree-odds") are pieces of beef or veal round steak prepared in the following way:

4 lbs. beef or veal rounds,	2 cups chopped tomatoes or
½" thick	1 (1-lb.) can tomatoes, mashed
½ cup bacon drippings	2 teaspoons salt
½ cup flour	1 cup red wine
1 cup chopped onions	1 cup water or tomato juice
2 cups chopped green onions	2 bay leaves
¾ cup chopped celery	½ teaspoon pepper
1½ cups chopped green peppers	2 tablespoons Worcestershire
2 cloves garlic, minced	16 drops Tabasco
½ teaspoon thyme	3 tablespoons chopped parsley

Cut meat in serving-size pieces. Pound with mallet to ¼" thickness. In large skillet, brown meat well in ¼ cup bacon grease. Remove to warm plate. To skillet add remainder of grease and flour. Stir and cook slowly to make a dark brown roux. Add onions, green onions, celery, green pepper, and garlic and saute until limp. Add thyme and tomatoes and cook 5 minutes. Return meat to skillet. Add salt, wine, water or tomato juice, and stir well. Add bay leaves, pepper, Worcestershire and Tabasco. Lower heat, stir, and cook covered about 2 hours. Remove bay leaves. Stir in parsley. Cool and let grillades sit several hours or overnight in refrigerator. You may add more liquid—you do not want this dish dry. Grillades should be very tender. Reheat before serving over hot grits or rice. Serves 8—10.

DIXIE OYSTERS

4 cups raw oysters	4 drops Tabasco
2 tablespoons parsley, minced	2 teaspoons lemon juice
2 tablespoons chopped green	1¼ cups bread crumbs
onions and tops	1½ sticks butter
¼ teaspoon each, salt and pepper	¾ cup milk
2 teaspoons Worcestershire	Dash cayenne pepper

Butter a 1½-quart shallow casserole. Put a layer of oysters in bottom. Sprinkle with parsley, green onions with tops, salt, pepper, Worcestershire, Tabasco, lemon juice, bread crumbs and dot with butter. Repeat layer. Just before baking, pour milk over all and dash with cayenne. Be sure to mix well with oysters. Bake in 325-degree oven 35 minutes. Serves 8.

HOT CURRIED FRUIT

1 (1-lb.) can Bartlett pears	1 stick real butter
1 (1-lb.) can apricots	¾ cup brown sugar
1 (1-lb.) can chunk pineapple	1 teaspoon curry powder
1 (6-oz.) jar Maraschino cherries	

Drain fruit thoroughly. Mix all together in a baking dish. Melt butter and add brown sugar and curry powder. Pour over fruit. Bake uncovered 1 hour in 325-degree oven. Serves 8.

ZIPPY SPINACH MADELEINE

2 pkgs. frozen chopped spinach	¾ teaspoon celery salt
4 tablespoons butter	¾ teaspoon garlic salt
2 tablespoons flour	½ teaspoon salt
2 tablespoons chopped onion	1 teaspoon Worcestershire
½ cup evaporated milk	Red pepper to taste
½ cup vegetable liquor	1 (6-oz.) roll Jalapeno cheese
½ teaspoon pepper	½ cup buttered bread crumbs

Cook spinach according to package directions. Drain and reserve liquor. Melt butter in saucepan over low heat. Add flour, stirring until blended and smooth, but not brown. Add onion and cook until soft. Add liquids slowly, stirring to prevent lumps. Cook until smooth and thick and continue stirring. Add seasonings and cheese which has been cut into small pieces. Stir until melted. Combine with cooked spinach. Put into a casserole dish and top with buttered bread crumbs. Bake at 350 degrees for 30 minutes. Serves 6.

STORE-SOME-MORE BISCUITS

This recipe makes enough mix for 4 dozen biscuits. Store and use whenever you're ready for some good, hot biscuits!

6 cups plain flour, sifted	1 cup vegetable shortening
1 tablespoon salt	1 stick margarine, softened
3 tablespoons baking powder	

Mix the first 3 ingredients well. Cut in shortening and margarine until the consistency of coarse cornmeal. Store in an airtight container.

2 cups biscuit mix	½ cup milk

Stir mix and milk together with a fork until dough clings together. Roll out on a floured board and cut into circles. Prick top of each biscuit with fork several times. Bake in preheated 450-degree oven 8–10 minutes or until lightly golden on top.

SOUTHERN PECAN PIE

1 (8-in.) pie shell
5 tablespoons butter
¾ cup firmly packed brown sugar
3 eggs

1 cup light corn syrup
1 cup broken pecans
1 teaspoon vanilla
¼ teaspoon salt

Partially bake pie shell 3–4 minutes. Cream together butter and sugar and beat in eggs one at a time. Stir in remaining ingredients and pour into partially baked crust. Bake in 375-degree oven 30 minutes.

MICROWAVE PECAN PIE

3 tablespoons butter or oleo
3 eggs, beaten
1 cup dark corn syrup
¼ cup firmly packed brown
   sugar

1½ teaspoons flour
1 teaspoon vanilla
1½ cups pecan halves
1 (9-in.) baked pastry shell,
   baked in glass pie pan

Microwave butter in a 2-cup glass measuring cup on high for 1½ minutes. Stir in eggs, corn syrup, sugar, flour and vanilla. Microwave at medium high 2 minutes. Stir in pecans. Pour filling into pie shell. Microwave at medium 15 to 20 minutes, or until sides feel firm. Center will be soft, but will firm while standing.

INDEX

Winning Apple Cake 65
Winning Sauce 65

HORS D'OEUVRES

Cheese Wreath 72
Festive Broccoli Dip 72
Green Tomato Pickle 61
Natchos 58
Shrimp Mold 71
Tamale Delights 58
Toasted Pecans 72
Tomato Aspic Canapes 71
Vegetable Platter With
   Curry Dip 72
Watermelon Rind Pickles 43

MEATS

Barbequed Hamburgers 49
Beaux's Beef Stroganoff 16
Beef Bourguignon 21
Beefy Mexican Cornbread 58
Easter Sunrise Ham 26
Grillades 74
Jon Marzette 55
Mr. Jigg's Veal Parmigiana 24
Official Brunswick Stew 10
Papa's Shish-Ka-Bob 36
Smoked Brisket With Sauce 70
Victory Pork Roast 64

POULTRY

Auld Lang Syne Chicken
   Spaghetti 8
Carved Smoked Turkey 70
Chicken Broccoli Filling 31
Deadline Chicken Singapore 28
Delta Dove 60
Firecracker Chicken 41
Jug Chicken-In-The-Oven 47
Kotopits (Chicken in Filo) 52
Traditional Turkey 66

SALADS

Anne's Coleslaw 42
Avocado-Grapefruit Salad 58

Circumstance Salad 32
Emperor Salad 36
Extravagant Asparagus Salad 28
Fresh Start Salad Bar 8
Frosty Pear Salad 47
Fruit Compote 60
Grecian Salad 53
Harvest Fruit Salad 67
Heart-Of-My-Heart Tomato
   Salad 38
Hodge-Podge Salad 55
Hot Curried Fruit 75
Mandarin Memory Salad 33
Old Glory Potato Salad 41
Romantic Raspberry Salad 17
Shamrock Salad 23
Super Bowl Spinach Salad 10
Temptation Waldorf Salad 26
Tomato Soup Salad 14
Vieux Carre Salad 44

SALAD DRESSINGS

Blender Mayonnaise 70
French Dressing 36
Mama's Commemorative Mayon-
   naise 42
Memory Dressing 33
"Pompy" Seed Dressing 32
Super Bowl Salad Dressing 10

SAUCES AND FILLINGS

Basket Barbeque Sauce 49
Bechamel Sauce 52
Firecracker Barbeque Sauce 41
Giblet Gravy 66
Romantic Topping 17
Spicy Mustard 70
Tomato Sauce 24
Tart Lemon Filling 34
Whiskey Sauce 37

SEAFOOD

Caribbean Shrimp A La
   Grace 13
Creath's Oysters Rockefeller 23
Crescent City Shrimp Creole 44

Delectable Crabmeat Quiche 38
Dixie Oysters 74
Queen-For-A-Day Crabmeat 33
Shrimp Mold 71

SOUPS

Bride's Consomme 38
Essence of Tomato Soup 16
French Onion Soup 20
Gazpacho 33

VEGETABLES

Baked Tomatoes Rockefeller 53
Beans Anchored in Bacon 14
Best Canned Baked Beans 50
Broiled Tomato Parmesan 31
California Vegetable Marinade 55
Candidates Sweet Potatoes 64
Captain's Potatoes 14
Cheese Casserole 26
Crowder Peas With Okra 42
Cupid's Asparagus Spears 17
Down Home Turnip Greens 64
Gobbler's Cornbread Dressing 67

Green Fettucine 23
Gridiron Grits 60
In-The-Red Tomatoes 29
Lazy Daze Green Beans 47
Merry Marinated Vegetables 9
Mexi-Beans 59
Milestone Marinated Tomatoes 20
Orange-Glazed Garden Carrots 27
Pilgrim's Peas With Water Chestnuts 68
Quick 'N Easy Stuffed Potatoes 47
Saturday Night Special Beans 49
Senator's Squash Casserole 65
Spinach Souffle 21
Spinach Stuffed Squash 29
Spring Broccoli With Lemon Rain 26
Sweet Potatoes in Orange Cups 67
TLC Asparagus With Lemon Butter Sauce 38
Terrific Tomatoes 34
Touchdown Tomatoes 60
Zippy Spinach Madeleine 75

"Best of the Best" Cookbook Series:	ISBN Suffix
Best of the Best from Tennessee $14.95	20-8
Best of the Best from Florida $14.95	16-X
Best of the Best from Louisiana $14.95	13-5
Best of the Best from Mississippi $14.95	19-4
Best of the Best from Kentucky $14.95	27-5
Best of the Best from Alabama $14.95	28-3
Best of the Best from Georgia $16.95	30-5
Best of the Best from Texas $16.95	14-3
Best of the Best from Texas (hardbound) $17.95	34-8
Best of the Best from North Carolina $14.95	38-0
Best of the Best from South Carolina $14.95	39-9
Best of the Best from Virginia $14.95	41-0

Other Quail Ridge Press Cookbooks:

The Little Gumbo Book (hardbound) $6.95	17-8
The Little Bean Book (hardbound) $9.95	32-1
Gourmet Camping (hardbound) $10.95	23-2
Lite Up Your Life $14.95	40-2
Hors D'Oeuvres Everybody Loves $5.95	11-9
The Seven Chocolate Sins $5.95	01-1
A Salad A Day $5.95	02-X
Quickies for Singles $5.95	03-8
Twelve Days of Christmas Cookbook $5.95	00-3
Country Mouse Cheese Cookbook $5.95	10-0

ISBN Prefix: 0-937552-
All books are plastic-ring bound unless noted otherwise.
To order by mail send cash, check, money order, or
VISA/MasterCard number with expiration date to:

QUAIL RIDGE PRESS
P. O. Box 123
Brandon, MS 39043

Please add $1.50 postage and handling for first book;
50¢ per additional book. Gift wrap with enclosed card
add $1.00. Mississippi residents add 6% sales tax.

To order by VISA or MasterCard:

1-800-343-1583

Write or call for free catalog of all QRP books plus a
complete description of all the cookbooks listed above.